Kinki Japanese

▪ Kinki Japanese ▪

THE DIALECTS & CULTURE
OF THE KANSAI REGION

▪

DC Palter & Kaoru Horiuchi

CHARLES E. TUTTLE COMPANY
Rutland, Vermont & Tokyo, Japan

This book is dedicated to the memory of those who died in
the Great Hanshin Earthquake of 1995.

Published by the Charles E. Tuttle Company, Inc.
of Rutland, Vermont & Tokyo, Japan
with editorial offices at
2-6 Suido, 1-chome, Bunkyo-ku, Tokyo 112

LCC Card No. 94-61422
ISBN 0-8048-2017-1

First edition, 1995

Illustrations by Hiroshi Satoh
Printed in Japan

▪ Contents ▪

■ Acknowledgments ■

If we listed by name all the people who have helped make this book possible, this section would probably be longer than the book itself. But there are certain people who went far beyond the call of duty, and we would like to give a special note of thanks here.

First of all, we need to thank the kind people at the Charles E. Tuttle Company who worked with us to publish the book, especially Sally Schwager. A special thanks also to our agent, Henry Marini, without whom this book would never have found a home. Two people, Satsuki Tsubota and Yuriko Tanaka, spent an inordinant amount of time tracking down information for us and correcting our drafts.

The most difficult section for us to write was on the differences between the Osaka dialect and those of other regions in Kansai. Much of this information was provided by Ryusuke Kitamura, Hiroaki Kitano, and Hide Takahashi. Additional information about the Hanshin Tigers was provided by Shinya Fujimoto, whose e-mail handle is "Takoyaki Master."

Other people who spent a considerable amount of time helping out with questions and editorial suggestions include Mr. and Mrs. Hirota, Yoshie Komuro, Mariko Matsumoto, Naohisa Matsumoto, Kumiko

Matsuyama, Masaki Nakajima, David Sandrich, Kayo Shinoda, Yuko Taishaku, Yasuyo Yamamoto, and Megumi Yoshioka.

To these and all the other people who have helped us, a big "Ōkini!"

DC Palter
Kaoru Horiuchi

◼ Introduction ◼

Maido, maido and welcome to Kinki Japan, the land of historic temples, beautiful *geiko*, majestic mountains, and a vibrant, growing economy. Kindly leave your shoes and Tokyo dialect by the door. Remember to open your mouth when you speak here. If you like, you can roll your *r*'s all the way down Mt. Rokko. The more expression in your voice, the better. Tell jokes. Go ahead, don't be afraid. You're among friends—this is Kansai.

If you've been here long, you have already noticed that nobody is speaking the Japanese you so diligently studied in classes and textbooks. But you're going to have to learn the language of the streets. Of course, you can continue speaking the so-called *hyōjungo*, standard Japanese, the language of poker-faced bureaucrats up in Tokyo, exactly as it is taught on NHK, but you'll bore everybody and you sure won't have a clue as to what people are saying to you.

We have written this book for people who, like us, despite years of studying Japanese, or even being a Japanese native, felt clueless when they moved to the Kinki region and wore out their dictionaries trying in vain to find the meaning of words like *honma, akan, shimota,* and *chau*.

9

Despite being the language spoken by every one of your honorable neighbors, including your teachers, it isn't taught in classes and there are no textbooks, tapes, or television shows to help master it. Yet, not only does learning the language make it possible to understand everyone else but Kansai-*ben* is also a more expressive language, a more enjoyable dialect to speak than Tokyo-*ben*. And although it may seem strange for a foreigner to speak Kansai-*ben* (like a Japanese person affecting a Cockney accent or an Alabama drawl), it works wonders in livening up conversations, even in Tokyo.

If you're living in the Kyoto-Osaka-Kobe area, we hope you will find this book an indispensable road map to the language surrounding you. If you live elsewhere in the Kinki region, you should find that nearly all of our explanations are applicable, but that each region's dialect has its own pronunciation, special words, and other peculiarities you will need to pick up by paying close attention to your neighbors' speech patterns. If you live elsewhere in the southern half of Honshū, such as Nagoya, Hiroshima, or Okayama, we expect you will also find this book useful, since the language spoken throughout the area has more in common with Kansai-*ben* than with *hyōjungo*. But you should listen carefully for differences, and may want to consider writing a book similar to this one yourself. If you live anywhere else in Japan or, God forbid, are still stuck in Tokyo, you can at least pretend to live in Kansai and lighten up those monotonous conversations.

So pour yourself a glass of beer or a cup of hot Nada sake, put on your Hanshin Tigers baseball cap, and learn to speak like a native.

Ganbatte na!

What Is Kinki?

The Kinki region of Japan, called Kinki Chihō 近畿地方 in Japanese, covers a wide region in the southern half of the main Honshū 本州 island. Although the area considered part of the Kinki region has varied through history, it is now legally defined as the two cities (*fu*, 府) of Osaka and Kyoto and the five prefectures (*ken*, 県) of Hyogo, Mie, Nara, Shiga, and Wakayama or, in less legal terms, the land south of Nagoya and north of Okayama. This region includes Osaka, Kyoto, Kobe, Nara, Akashi, the Ise Peninsula, and Awaji Island. Of course, there are differences in the language across such a large area containing such drastic contrasts in living styles and history, but these local variations are all considered sub-dialects of Kansai-*ben*.

What then is Kansai? Although the word "Kansai" is used much more frequently than "Kinki," unfortunately the meaning of Kansai is somewhat muddled. Officially, Kansai is synonymous with Kinki, but in actual usage it usually applies only to the Kyoto-Osaka-Kobe area. This tri-city region is usually abbreviated in Japanese as Kei-Han-Shin 京阪神 , taking one character from the name of each city. Kei-Han-Shin also includes the suburban cities in between, such as Ibaragi, Hirakata, and Nishinomiya.

To make matters even more confusing, the version of Kansai-*ben* spoken in Osaka is often referred to as Osaka-*ben*, but as most outsiders cannot tell the difference, and because Osaka is by far the largest city in the region, quite often anyone who uses words such as *akan* and *honma* is considered to be speaking Osaka-*ben*.

For the purpose of this book, we consider all the variations of Japanese spoken throughout the Kinki region to be part of Kansai-*ben*, and have tried to indicate the words or phrases that are used only in Osaka or only in the Kei-Han-Shin area.

We would also like to note that although many other areas of Central, Southern, and Western Honshū, such as Nagoya, Okayama, and

Hiroshima, are not considered to be part of the Kinki region, the language in these areas has more in common with Kansai-*ben* than with standard Japanese. We have therefore tried to make this book useful for people living in these regions as well.

The Dialect

Why does the language spoken in Kansai differ from that in Tokyo and even vary from place to place within Kansai, even within the city of Osaka? The reason lies in the fact that before the advent of modern transportation and communication, residents of each area had little contact with people from more than a few miles away. As the language grew and changed, it did so within the confines of each locality. With the advent of modern communications, as well as the centralization of power in Tokyo, nearly everyone in Japan became able to understand and speak the officially sanctioned version of Japanese (the Tokyo version, of course). Regional dialects, however, although diminishing in usage, are still a fact of life in Japan. Children still master the local dialect spoken by parents and friends long before they are taught to speak standard Japanese.

But why are some words used in Kansai while different words with nearly identical meanings are used in Tokyo, and why are certain pronunciations of the same word favored in Kansai over the standard pronunciation? Essentially, it is because that is the way it is, but there are a few guiding rules for newcomers to Kansai-*ben*.

• Many words in standard Japanese are contracted. Note the following examples.

KANSAI	STANDARD	ENGLISH
yō よう	*yoku* よく	very, well

omoroi おもろい	*omoshiroi* 面白い	interesting
chau ちゃう	*chigau* 違う	wrong
kora こら	*kore wa* これは	this is
sora そら	*sore wa* それは	that is

• For no reason other than history, certain words are used in Kansai while others are used in Tokyo.

nukui ぬくい	*atatakai* 暖かい	warm
kosobai こそばい	*kusuguttai* くすぐったい	ticklish
kokeru こける	*korobu* 転ぶ	fall down
hokasu ほかす	*suteru* 捨てる	throw away

• "S" sounds in standard Japanese are often replaced by "h" sounds.

-han −はん	*-san* −さん	Mr., Ms., Mrs., Miss
-mahen −まへん	*-masen* −ません	(negative conjugation)
-mahyō −まひょう	*-mashō* −ましょう	("let's do" conjugation)

• *Desu* です and its variations are replaced by *ya* や.

ya や	*da* だ	is
yaro やろ	*darō* だろう	don't you think?
yakara やから	*dakara* だから	therefore

• Long vowels, especially at the end of words, are often shortened.

iko 行こ	*ikō* 行こう	let's go
sho しょ	*shō* しょう	let's do
soya そや, *seya* せや	*sō da* そうだ	yes

• Short vowels at the end of words are sometimes lengthened.

tē 手え	*te* 手	hand
kē 毛え	*ke* 毛	hair

KANSAI	STANDARD	ENGLISH
kā 蚊あ	*ka* 蚊	mosquito
kii 木い	*ki* 木	tree
chii 血い	*chi* 血	blood
tō 戸お	*to* 戸	door

• Double consonants (denoted by *tsu* っ) are often softened or replaced with a long vowel.

tsukōte つこうて , *tsukote* つこて	*tsukatte* 使って	use
kōta 買うた	*katta* 買った	bought
morota もろた , *mōta* もうた	*moratta* もらった	received
yūte ゆうて	*itte* 言って	say

• The final vowel of words ending with two vowels, especially adjectives that end in -*i*, are dropped in informal conversations and the final sound lengthened for emphasis. Stronger emphasis is indicated by longer sounds.

EMPHASIZED	STANDARD KANSAI	ENGLISH
shindo— しんど〜	*shindoi* しんどい	tiring
omoro— おもろ〜	*omoroi* おもろい	interesting
gottsu— ごっつ〜	*gottsui* ごっつい	very
atsu— あつ〜	*atsui* 暑い	hot
ita— いた〜	*itai* 痛い	painful
kusa— 臭〜	*kusai* 臭い	smelly

• Although the level of formality depends on the person, place, and situation, in general the language in Kansai is less formal than in Tokyo. Typical conversations among Kinki people sound a notch less formal than those among Tokyoites, who consider this to be more an expression of bad manners than friendliness. Of course, there are large gradations in formality in Kansai-*ben* as well as in standard Japanese, and it is important to speak with the correct level of formality in each situation. Women tend to speak more politely and use more standard Japanese than men.

• Kansai-*ben* speakers often repeat the same word twice. This is especially common when showing sympathy or relieving someone's anxiety.

| *kamahen, kamahen* | かまへん、かまへん | I don't mind at all. |
| *chau, chau* | ちゃう、ちゃう | No, that's not right. |

• Accentuation of words also differs, but it is difficult to give any rules other than to recommend listening to your neighbors instead of language tapes, especially as there are large variations even within Kansai. Here are some examples of how pronunciation in Kansai differs from Tokyo.

The most often cited example is the homonym *ame*, which can mean either rain 雨 , or candy 飴 . In Kansai, the word for rain is accented on the second syllable *a-ME,* and the word for candy is unaccented *a-me.* In Tokyo, the accentuation is on the first syllable *A-me* for rain and on the second syllable *a-ME* for candy. Here are a few more examples:

KANSAI	TOKYO	KANJI	ENGLISH
a-ME	*A-me*	雨	rain
a-me	*a-ME*	飴	candy
HA-shi	*ha-shi*	橋	bridge
ha-shi	*HA-shi*	箸	chopsticks
I-nu	*i-NU*	犬	dog
DE-n-sha	*de-n-sha*	電車	train
o-ha-YO-u	*o-HA-YOU*	お早う	good morning
FU-ku	*fu-KU*	服	clothes
KU-tsu	*ku-TSU*	靴	shoes
bu-SU	*BU-su*	ぶす	ugly
chu-U-ka	*CHU-u-ka*	中華	Chinese food
na-n-DE?	*NA-n-de?*	何で	why?

Accentuation is, in general, much stronger in Kansai than in Tokyo, where pronunciation is basically flat. For example, *fuku* has a barely perceptible accent on the second syllable in Tokyo, so it is listed as *fu-KU,* but the accent on the first syllable in Kansai is relatively strong. This gives the speech in Kansai its more melodic, emotional tone as opposed to flat, monotonic Tokyo speech.

▪ 1 ▪
Fifteen Words Needed
to Survive in Kansai

This first set of fifteen terms (ten words and five grammatical expressions), we believe, are the most critical for understanding the language around you. If you can master the usage of these words, you will be recognized by everyone as a Kansai resident.

VOCABULARY

1. *ahō, aho* 阿呆、あほ
2. *akan* あかん
3. *chau* ちゃう
4. *ē* ええ
5. *honma* ほんま
6. *maido* 毎度
7. *metcha, mutcha* めっちゃ、むっちゃ
8. *nanbo* なんぼ
9. *ōkini* 大きに
10. *oru* おる

GRAMMATICAL EXPRESSIONS

11. *-haru* ーはる
12. *-hen* ーへん
13. *nen* ねん
14. *shimota, mota* しもた、もた
15. *ya* や

1. *ahō, aho*　阿呆、アホ　fool, foolish, stupid

Although considered a part of standard Japanese, *ahō*, or *aho,* is used often only in Kansai. While it is sometimes written in kanji as 阿呆, pronounced *ahō*, the final vowel sound is often clipped off and it is usually written in katakana as *aho* アホ. Depending on the tone and particle used with *aho*, the word can range in meaning from a playful way to say "no" to a fairly strong expletive. Women as well as men use this word, but women need to pay special attention to usage and tone in order to avoid sounding unladylike. Women usually avoid saying *aho* directly to the person they are criticizing.

Nande kono hon no ichiban saisho ni, konna aho na kotoba iretan?
Omaera, aho ya nā.
なんでこの本の一番最初に、こんなアホな言葉入れたん?
お前ら、アホやなあ。
Why did you put such a stupid word at the beginning of this book?
You guys are pretty stupid.

Omaera is the plural of *omae* (see word entry 43) and is used by men to mean "you." *Ya* replaces *da* だ. (See 15)

We agree it is somewhat reckless of us to begin your new vocabulary with *aho,* but of the fifteen most important words in Kansai-*ben*, this one ended up first in alphabetical order and second only to *akan* in A-I-U order. We are too *aho* to come up with a better system, so please don't stop reading now.

SUZUKI:	*Kondo, anta toko no yome-han to dēto sasetē ya.*
HONDA:	*Nani aho na koto yūten nen!*
鈴木:	今度、あんたとこの嫁はんとデートさせてえや。
本田:	何アホなこと言うてんねん!

Nani aho na Koto yūten nen!

Anta toko no yome-han to dēto sasetē ya.

SUZUKI: Do you mind if I take your wife out on a date?
HONDA: Don't say such stupid things!

-Tēya ーてえや is used when making requests in very casual situations and is conjugated to the *-te* ーて form of the verb. *-Tēna* ーてえな has the same meaning. *Toko* とこ is the Kansai version of *tokoro* 所. (See 53)

HIRAKATA:	*Kondo no bōnasu sanjuppāsento katto yate!*
IBARAGI:	*Sonna aho na. Kaisha nani kangaeten nen?*
枚方：	今度のボーナス30％カットやて！
茨木：	そんなアホな。会社何考えてんねん？
HIRAKATA:	We're getting a 30% cut in our next bonus!
IBARAGI:	How can they be so stupid? What is this company thinking?

Kangaeten nen is equivalent to *kangaete iru* 考えている. *-Ten nen* is the Kansai version of *-te iru,* the progressive verb (-ing form) conjugation. (See 45)

2. *akan* あかん   bad, useless, impossible, no

Akan is a very distinctive and easily recognizable feature of the language spoken in Kansai. Although not vulgar, this word is considered to be somewhat impolite. *Akan* is probably a modified version of *ikan*, which is the clipped form of *ikenai*, meaning "must not" or "cannot." *Akan* has many uses, both by itself and as a part of grammatical expressions. Its various meanings, somewhat similar to *dame* 駄目 in standard Japanese, are explained below.

(a) no! impossible!

SUZUKI:	*Issen man en, kashite kurehen?*
HONDA:	*Akan!*
鈴木：	一千万円、貸してくれへん？
本田：	あかん！
SUZUKI:	Can you loan me 10 million yen?
HONDA :	NO!

(b) expletive

MITSUI:	*Anta no kabu, hanbun ni sagatta de.*
ITOH:	*Akan.*
三井：	あんたの株、半分に下がったで。
伊藤：	あかん。
MITSUI:	The value of your stock fell by half.
ITOH:	#&%$!

In this case, although *akan* is used as an expletive, it has more of a tone of regret than anger. *Anta* あんた is an informal word for "you." It is a contracted form of *anata* あなた, but is much more informal. It is used by both men and women, as opposed to *omae* お前, which is a rougher word for "you" used only by men.

ANNOUNCER: *Hanshin, hōmuran utaremashita.*

TORAKICHI: *Akan.*

アナウンサー: 阪神、ホームラン打たれました。

トラキチ: あかん。

ANNOUNCER: A home run was hit off of Hanshin.

TORAKICHI: #&%$!

(c) no good, bad

MIKA: *Shiken donai yatta?*

TOMOKO: *Akankatta wa.*

美香: 試験どないやった?

友子: あかんかったわ。

MIKA: How was the test?

TOMOKO: Miserable.

Tomoko obviously should have studied harder. *Donai yatta* どない やった means "how was it?" *Akankatta* is the past tense of *akan*.

(d) don't do that!

DAUGHTER:	*Hona, ite kuru wa.*
MOTHER:	*Akan yo.*
娘：	ほな、行て来るわ。
母：	あかんよ。
DAUGHTER:	I'm going out now.
MOTHER:	No you're not.

This usage is heard quite often when parents are telling their children what they are not allowed to do.

KENSUKE:	*Kono butaman, kutte ē?*
KYŌTA:	*Akan de.*
健助：	この豚マン、食ってええ？
京太：	あかんで。
KENSUKE:	Can I eat this pork roll?
KYŌTA:	No!

Note that this example is typical of male speech only. Women use *taberu* 食べる instead of *kuu* 食う for the verb "to eat." *Akan,* especially followed by the particle *de,* sounds rough and in female speech would probably be followed by *yo* instead.

The same conversation between two women might be as follows:

MIKA:	*Sono butaman tabete mo ē?*
TOMOKO:	*Akan yo.*
美香：	その豚マン食べてもええ？
友子：	あかんよ。

Akan nen and *akande* are also often used to mean "no" or "you can't."

(e) must (used as a double negative)

Atarashii kuruma, kawana akan.

新しい車、買わなあかん。

I've got to buy a new car.

Shinbun yomana akan.

新聞読まなあかん。

I have to read the newspaper.

In this usage, the verb is conjugated as the standard negative form (i.e., *-nai*) with the final *-i* sound clipped off and followed by *akan*. This structure is identical in meaning to the *-nakereba naranai* form, but is much more colloquial. *Suru* is usually conjugated as *sena akan* せな あかん.

Shigoto sena akan.

仕事せなあかん。

I've got to work.

3. chau　　ちゃう　　(a) no, different, wrong; (b) isn't that right?

(a) *Chau* is the clipped form of *chigau* 違う. This contraction is widely used throughout Kansai in place of *chigau*.

chau de	ちゃうで	you're wrong
chau, chau	ちゃう、ちゃう	that's wrong

KENSUKE: 　*Denshadai nihyaku en ya na.*

KYŌTA: 　*Chau, chau. Nihyaku gojū en yade.*

健助 : 　電車代二百円やな。

京太 : 　ちゃう、ちゃう。二百五十円やで。

KENSUKE: 　The train fare is 200 yen, right?

KYŌTA: 　No, it's 250 yen.

Because *chau* is a verb ending in *-u,* it can be conjugated to *chaimasu* ちゃいます for slightly more formal situations.

KAKARICHŌ: 　*Omae no happyō, daiseikō yattan chau?*

HIRASHAIN: 　*Zannen nagara, chaimasu wa.*

係長 : 　お前の発表、大成功やったんちゃう？

平社員 : 　残念ながら、ちゃいますわ。

BOSS: 　Your presentation was a big hit, right?

EMPLOYEE: 　No, unfortunately not.

Yatta is the Kansai version of *datta* だった.

(b) In the first line of the above dialogue and in the following examples, *chau* is used in a manner similar to a sentence-ending particle meaning "isn't that right?" The standard equivalent is *janai?* じゃない？ or *sō ja nai?* そうじゃない？

Are, Nozomi chau?
あれ、望ちゃう？
Isn't that Nozomi?

Mō ē chau?
もうええちゃう？
That's enough already, don't you think?

Sore de jūbun yattan chau?
それで十分やったんちゃう？
That was good enough, right?

4. *ē* ええ good, that's enough
Ē replaces *ii* いい, which usually means "good," but can mean "no" or "that's enough" or just about anything else depending on the context. Although usually written as *ē* ええ, the pronunciation is actually between *ē* and *ei*. *Ē* can be used anytime *ii* is used in standard Japanese. It is used extensively in Kansai and throughout much of the southern half of Honshū. But don't confuse this with the *ē* that means "yes," which is used throughout Japan.

Ano kuruma, kakko ē nā.
あの車、かっこええなあ。
That's a pretty car.

Kakko かっこ is a contraction of *kakkō* 格好, which means "appearance" or "shape," and is often used with *ē* to denote something that looks good, or with *warui* or *waru* for something ugly. By changing the order, however, we get the word *ēkakkoshii* ええ格好しい, which means pretentious, something very much disliked in Kansai.

Like *ii*, *ē* preceding a noun is a very common pattern.

Ē tenki ya nā.
ええ天気やなあ。
Nice weather, isn't it.

Ē fuku yaro.
ええ服やろ。
Nice clothes, huh.

The following sentences have the same meaning of "I've had enough already" or "stop it already," but the last of the three examples is the strongest.

Ē kagen ni shitokiya!	ええ加減にしときや！
Ē kagen ni shii ya!	ええ加減にしいや！
Ē kagen ni sei!	ええ加減にせい！

Just like *ii*, *ē*, especially when following *mō* もう, means "no" or "no thanks."

Mō ē もうええ means "I've had enough" (when turning down an offer of food, etc.) or "I give up" (especially when talking to oneself). This is often followed by *wa*.

HIKARI:	*Ē fuku ya nā.*
NOZOMI:	*Kōtara?*
HIKARI:	*Ē wa. Takai kara.*
光：	ええ服やなあ。
望：	こうたら？
光：	ええわ。高いから。

HIKARI: These are nice clothes, huh?

NOZOMI: Why don't you buy them?

HIKARI: Naa. They're too expensive.

5. *honma*   ほんま   really

Honma is equivalent to *hontō* 本当, meaning "really." It is often used to indicate that the person is still listening to what the speaker is saying.

Honma ni?	ほんまに？	Really?
Honma, honma.	ほんま、ほんま。	Really, really.
Honma ya!	ほんまや！	Really!
Honma kainā.	ほんまかいなあ。	You're joking.

    Honma ni, like *hontō ni,* is also often used as an adverb to strengthen the word following it.

Kyō, honma ni atsui nā.
今日、ほんまに暑いなあ。
It's really hot today.

Sono nēchan, honma ni kirei ya nen.
そのねえちゃん、ほんまに奇麗やねん。
That girl's really beautiful.

Honma or *honma ni* will be heard at least ten times per minute in a typical conversation as far south as Okayama, but this word is very distinctive and, because of the frequency of its use, is among the most recognizable features of Kinki Japanese.

6. maido　毎度　hello

Maido translates literally as "every time" but, as with the all-purpose *dōmo* どうも, *maido* can represent *maido arigatō gozaimasu,* meaning "thank you for your patronage" or other stock phrases of greeting. In actual usage, *maido* is probably best translated as "hello" but is often used as a part of expressions of thanks. Although it is arguably the penultimate Kansai-*ben* word, in actuality it isn't used much by young people, especially outside of Osaka. *Maido* is often combined with *ōkini*.

Maido, ōkini.
毎度、大きに。
Thanks for your patronage.

Ā, maido maido.
ああ、まいど まいど。
Hello/ Thanks for calling/ Thanks for coming.

This last example is usually used by the person receiving a phone call in the office after the caller has identified himself. However, as Kansai-*ben* is looked down upon by callers from Tokyo, including the corporate head-office personnel, the more acceptable *dōmo, dōmo* is often substituted when the caller is neither a close friend nor another native of Osaka.

7. metcha, mutcha　めっちゃ、むっちゃ　very

Both *metcha* and *mutcha* are adverbs meaning "very." In usage, they are similar to *totemo* とても, *taihen* 大変, or *sugoku* すごく. *Metcha* and *mutcha* are completely interchangeable and can be thought of as variations in pronunciation of the same word.

Metcha omoroi.
めっちゃおもろい。
Very interesting.

Mutcha umai.
むっちゃうまい。
Very delicious.

Metcha hagaii.
めっちゃはがいい。
Very irritating.

8. *nanbo* なんぼ how much

Nanbo is a distinctive Kansai word used in the entire southern half of Honshū, including Hiroshima and Okayama, in place of *ikura* いくら. *Nanbo* by itself means "how much?" when inquiring about a price. The standard *ikura . . . -temo* expression, meaning "no matter how much . . ." can also be replaced by *nanbo . . . -temo.*

SUMIYOSHI:	*Sore nanbo?*
SAKAI:	*Sen en.*
住吉：	それ、なんぼ？
堺：	千円。
SUMIYOSHI:	How much is that?
SAKAI:	1,000 yen.

Tōkyō no honsha ni nanbo setsumei shite mo, wakatte kurehen.

東京の本社になんぼ説明しても、分かってくれへん。

No matter how much I try explaining to the Tokyo head office, they fail to understand.

9. *ōkini*　大きに　thank you

Like *maido*, *ōkini* is another typical Kansai word that isn't used that often in Kansai anymore. Its use seems centered in Kyoto, where it is always used in place of *dōmo* or *arigatō* by nearly everyone. In Osaka, the use of this word is limited mostly to older people, and *dōmo* or *arigatō* are heard just as often as *ōkini*. In Kobe, its use is limited to old men and women shopkeepers. However, because *ōkini* is understood and recognized by everyone as proper Kansai-*ben*, even though the Tokyo mentality has been partially successful in converting most people to using *dōmo*, we recommend you say *ōkini*, at least occasionally, to the bus or taxi driver when he drops you off or to the clerk who gives you change. If you live in Kyoto, forget about saying *dōmo* or *arigatō* outside of Japanese classes.

Note that the pronunciation of *ōkini* differs somewhat for men and women. Women lift their voice slightly on the middle syllable *(ō-KI-ni)* while men accent the first syllable *(Ō-ki-ni)*.

10. *oru*　おる　is, exists (for humans and animals)

The use of *oru* in place of *iru* is widespread not only throughout all of Kansai but everywhere in the southern half of Japan. Because *oru* is used as the humble version of *iru* in standard Japanese, however, and as such is only used to refer to oneself, the use of *oru* in referring to other people seems rude to non-natives of Kansai.

HIRASHAIN:　*Ashita oraremasu ka?*
KAKARICHŌ:　*Suman kedo, ashita orehen wa.*

平社員：　　明日おられますか？

係長：　　　すまんけど、明日おれへんわ。

EMPLOYEE:　Will you be in tomorrow?

BOSS:　　　Sorry, I'm going to be out tomorrow.

As in standard Japanese, the passive *-rareru* form of the verb is often used to make the sentence more formal, especially when asking something about your conversation partner. Therefore, *oraremasu ka?* is heard quite often in place of *irasshaimasu ka?* especially in business telephone conversations and in the office. As this is an honorific form, it cannot be used when referring to oneself.

Suman すまん is one of the Kansai versions of *sumimasen* すみません. This is the most clipped form and the least polite. *Sunmahen* すんまへん is slightly more polite and is considered "correct" Kansai-*ben*. In some parts of Kansai it is considered rude and is thus used mostly by men and older people. Two versions that are also used widely are *sunmasen* すんません and *suimasen* すいません.

Note that the employee speaks more formally to the boss than the boss does when he answers the employee. The employee uses *oraremasu* while the boss uses *orehen*.

In addition to its use as a stand-alone verb, *oru* can also replace *iru* as an auxiliary verb to create the progressive form of the verb. *-Te oru* is usually contracted to *-toru*.

Nani shitoru?
何しとる？
What are you doing?

11. *-haru* 　ーはる　 (honorific verb conjugation)

This verb conjugation forms an integral part of Kinki's *keigo* 敬語 , the extra polite language used to show respect to people of higher rank or to strangers. However, as Kansai-*ben* generally has a reputation of being less formal than standard Japanese, when truly formal language is required, such as during job interviews or intercom announcements, standard formal Japanese is usually used. Therefore, the *-haru* form is most often heard in situations that fall somewhere between formal and informal. It is used especially by women, since they are expected to speak somewhat formally to male acquaintances but don't wish to sound cold by speaking too formally. It is also a convenient form for a company's younger employees when speaking to or about senior members, since it shows respect without sounding like excessive bootlicking. This form is used often in Kyoto, where it is considered a part of standard speech rather than *keigo*.

This conjugation is believed to have been derived by shortening *nasaru* to *-haru*. However, unlike *nasaru*, *-haru* can be used with nearly any verb to make it more formal.

In most places in Kansai, the *-haru* form is conjugated to the *-i* base of the verb. However, in Kyoto and surrounding areas, such as Nara, conjugation with the *-a* base of the verb is more common.

Where are you going?

Doko e ikiharun desu ka?   どこへ行きはるんですか？

Doko e ikiharimasu ka?   どこへ行きはりますか？

Doko e ikaharun desu ka? (Kyoto) どこへ行かはるんですか？（京都）

As in standard Japanese, a sentence in the polite form can end in either the *-masu* conjugation of the verb *(-harimasu)* or by affixing *-n desu (-harun desu).* The meaning of all three sentences above is essentially the same.

Nani tabeharimasu ka?
何食べはりますか？
What would you like to eat?

The *-haru* form can also be attached to the *-te* ーて form of the verb to create the -ing form.

Doko e itteharun desu ka?
どこへ行ってはるんですか？
Where is he going?

Sensei, nani yūtehattan?
先生、何ゆうてはったん？
What was the teacher saying?

12. *-hen* ーへん (negative verb conjugation)

The verb conjugation *-hen* is similar in usage to *-nai. -Hen* is attached to either the *-a* base or *-e* base of verbs in order to form the negative of verbs. It can also be attached to the *-e* base to produce the negative "cannot" form of verbs. For example, the verb *yomu* 読む (to read) in standard Japanese is conjugated *yomanai* 読まない, meaning "not read," or *yomenai* 読めない, meaning "can't read." In Kansai, *yomu* is conjugated *yomahen* 読まへん, meaning "not read," or *yomehen* 読めへん, meaning either "not read" or "can't read." Which of the two meanings is intended can only be determined from the context. However, when intending to say unequivocally "can't read," *yomu* can also be conjugated *yomarehen* 読まれへん.

To make the negative past tense, conjugate the verb with *-henkatta* in the same manner as *-hen*. For example, the past tense of *ikahen* 行かへん, "don't go," is *ikahenkatta* 行かへんかった, "didn't go."

yomu	読む	to read
yomahen	読まへん	don't read
yomehen	読めへん	can't read, don't read
yomarehen	読まれへん	can't read
yomahenkatta	読まへんかった	didn't read
yomehenkatta	読めへんかった	couldn't read, didn't read
yomarehenkatta	読まれへんかった	couldn't read
iku	行く	to go
ikahen	行かへん	won't go
ikehen	行けへん	can't go, won't go
ikarehen	行かれへん	can't go
ikahenkatta	行かへんかった	didn't go
ikehenkatta	行けへんかった	couldn't go, didn't go
ikarehenkatta	行かれへんかった	couldn't go

Here are a few more examples. Because the *-e* base conjugation is more common than the *-a* base form, only the *-e* form is shown, but most verbs can be conjugated to either base.

taberu 食べる	*tabehen* 食べへん	don't eat
dekiru 出来る	*dekehen* でけへん	can't do
kamau 構う	*kamehen* かめへん	don't mind
wakaru 分かる	*wakarehen* 分かれへん	don't understand

Kuru 来る and *suru* する have two forms, one where *-hen* is changed to *-hin*.

kuru	来る	to come
kēhen	けえへん	don't come
kiihin	きいひん	don't come
korarehen	こられへん	can't come
suru	する	to do
sēhen	せえへん	don't do
shiihin	しいひん	don't do

13. *nen* ねん (neutral sentence ending)

Sentence-ending particles, or *gobi* 語尾, are a Japanese grammatical form with no real equivalent in English, but, as only one minute listening to any Japanese conversation will prove, their use must be mastered in order to speak like a native. The purpose of these words, which have no intrinsic meaning, is to control the mood or tone of the sentence, something English speakers generally accomplish by changing pitch, speed, and accentuation. Some examples include the pervasive *ne, na,* and *yo,* but, as you might expect, these sentence endings differ by dialect. You may have already noticed that the sentence endings in the examples up until now differ from those used in Tokyo. As they are one of the main points differentiating Kansai-*ben* from other dialects, a number of common sentence endings will be introduced in the following pages.

Nen is one of the most typical and frequently used sentence endings in the Kansai region. *Nen* is essentially neutral in tone, and is used when eliciting response from the conversation partner. It also has the effect of ending the sentence in a smooth manner. When used by itself, it has a somewhat soft tone, but is sometimes followed by stronger endings, such as *de*, for emphasis.

Suki ya nen.	好きやねん。	I like it.
So ya nen.	そやねん。	It's true.
Makudo iku nen.	マクド行くねん。	I'm going to McDonalds.
Baito yamen nen de!	バイト辞めんねんで！	I'm quitting my part-time job!

14. *shimota, mota*　しもた、もた　completely
Shimota is the local version of *shimatta,* which roughly translates as "completely," but with a variety of usages dependent on context. When used as a stand-alone verb, the final *a* is sometimes lengthened to *shimota*— しもた〜 for extra emphasis. In conjugated form, *shimota* is often clipped to *mota.*

(a) Used usually under one's breath as an expletive indicating contempt for one's own mistakes.

Shimota! Mō osoi wa.
しもた！もう遅いわ。
#&%$! I'm late.

(b) Following the *-te* form of a verb, *shimota* indicates action completely finished or strengthens the preceding verb.

Mō densha, itte shimota.
もう電車、行ってしもた。
The train's already gone.

Sanzen en mo, tsukote shimota.
三千円も、つこてしもた。
I used up 3,000 yen.

    Tsukote is the Kansai pronunciation for *tsukatte* 使って. In this context, *shimota* is often contracted to *mota* もた, especially in less formal situations. This is similar to the Tokyo contraction of *shimatta* to *chatta*.

Mō densha, itte mota.　　　　　　　もう電車、行ってもた。
Sanzen en mo tsukote mota.　　　　三千円もつこてもた。

15. *ya* や is

Ya replaces *da* だ, the informal version of *desu* です. Similarly, note the following:

yaro	やろ	replaces *darō*	だろう
yan	やん	replaces *janai*	じゃない
yanka	やんか	replaces *janai ka*	じゃないか
yattara	やったら	replaces *dattara*	だったら

    Ya and its variations are arguably the most critical difference in grammar between standard Japanese and Kansai-*ben*. Its usage is so pervasive and noticeable that Tokyo-based novelists, when trying to portray a character from Kansai, merely change every *da* to *ya* in the characters' dialogue.

The usage of *ya* is varied and can only be explained effectively through examples.

KANSAI	STANDARD	ENGLISH
uso ya 嘘や	*uso da* 嘘だ	you're kidding
iya ya いやや	*iya da* いやだ	yuck
so yattara そやったら	*sō dattara* そうだったら	if that's true
ittan ya 行ったんや	*ittan da* 行ったんだ	went
suki ya 好きや	*suki da* 好きだ	I like it
so yaro そやろ	*sō darō* そうだろう	don't you think so?
nan ya? 何や？	*nan da?* 何だ？	what?
so yanka そやんか	*sō janai ka* そうじゃないか	isn't it?
so yanke そやんけ	*sō janai ka* そうじゃないか	isn't it? (men only)

▪ 2 ▪

Example Conversations I

Conversation 1: Between two female college students.

1	TOMOKO:	*Nani shiten non?*
2	MIKA:	*Shukudai shiten nen.*
3	TOMOKO:	*Hona, konban no pātii ikehen non?*
4	MIKA:	*Ikitai nen kedo nā . . . Akan nen.*
5	TOMOKO:	*Ē yan, iko.*

1	友子：	何してんのん？
2	美香：	宿題してんねん。
3	友子：	ほな、今晩のパーティー行けへんのん？
4	美香：	行きたいねんけどなあ . . . あかんねん。
5	友子：	ええやん、行こ。

1	TOMOKO:	What are you doing?
2	MIKA:	I'm doing my homework.
3	TOMOKO:	Then I guess you won't be coming to the party tonight.

39

4 MIKA: I want to go, but . . . No, I can't.
5 TOMOKO: Forget about the homework. Let's go!

Line 1: The final *non* softens the sentence and asks for a response. *No* の is the standard Japanese equivalent. (See 59)

Line 3: *Hona* is equivalent to *sore ja* それじゃ, meaning "if that is true." (See 18) The negative of *iku* 行く (to go) is conjugated as *ikehen* 行けへん meaning "won't go" or "can't go." *Non* is often used at the end of a sentence, especially when asking a question. It is softer than *ka* and is used particularly by women.

Line 4: *Nā* なあ is used when asking oneself a question or expressing a wish. (See 28) *Akan* in this case has the same meaning as *dame*, or that it is impossible for her to go.

Line 5: *Ē yan* would be equivalent to *ii janai* いいじゃない. It is impossible to translate this expression directly into English, but in this case it means "that's already good enough" or "don't worry about it." The standard *ikō* 行こう is shortened to *iko* 行こ in Kansai.

Conversation 2: Between a male customer and a shopkeeper at a market in Nankō.

1 SUMIYOSHI: *Uwā, kore metcha ē nā.*
2   *Otchan, kore nanbo?*
3 SAKAI: *Sen en yakedo.*
4 SUMIYOSHI: *Accha—! Shimota—!*
5   *Kyūhyaku en shika arahen wa.*
6 SAKAI: *Hona, kyūhyaku en ni shitoku wa.*
7 SUMIYOSHI: *Honma? Ōkini.*
8 SAKAI: *Ōkini.*

1	住吉：	うわあ、これめっちゃええなあ。
2		おっちゃん、これなんぼ？
3	堺：	千円やけど。
4	住吉：	あっちゃあ〜！しもた〜！
5		九百円しかあらへんわ。
6	堺：	ほな、九百円にしとくわ。
7	住吉：	ほんま？大きに。
8	堺：	大きに。

1	SUMIYOSHI:	Wow, this is really nice.
2		How much is it?
3	SAKAI:	That's 1,000 yen.
4	SUMIYOSHI:	Damn!
5		I've only got 900 yen.
6	SAKAI:	In that case, I'll give it to you for 900 yen.
7	SUMIYOSHI:	Really? Thanks.
8	SAKAI:	Thank you.

Line 1: *Metcha*, meaning "very," is used to intensify *ē*, meaning "good." Sumiyoshi ends his sentences with *nā* when he talks to himself.

Line 2: *Otchan* is short for *ojisan* おじさん, meaning "uncle." It is used to address a middle-aged man and is informal but friendly rather than rude. *Ossan* おっさん is also used as a contraction for *ojisan,* but is considered rude and would not be used when addressing someone, except as an insult or a joke. *Nanbo* is used to ask the price.

Line 4: *Shimota*— is an expression of annoyance at his own mistake of not having enough money with him to buy it.

Line 5: *Arahen* is the negative of *aru.* Tokyoites would say *nai* instead. *Wa* is used to soften the sentence ending. Although in standard Japanese *wa* is used almost exclusively by women, in Kansai it is used just as much by men when adding a slight touch of politeness to the sentence. (See 30)

Line 6: Here *hona* means "in that case." *Shitoku*, a contraction of the *shite oku* form of *suru,* is often used in Kansai to indicate doing a favor for the other person.

Line 8: *Ōkini* is used quite often by elderly shopkeepers.

Conversation 3: Between a department chief and one of his employees.

1	HIRASHAIN:	*Buchō, ashita oraremasu ka?*
2	BUCHŌ:	*Oru omou kedo, chotto shirabete miru wa.*
3		*Ah, akan wa, ashita orahen wa. Nande?*
4	HIRASHAIN:	*Ano, Takagi-san ashita kotchi ni kuru te yūteharun desu kedo.*
5	BUCHŌ:	*Eh? Ashita, Takagi mo onaji kaigi ni derun ya de.*
6		*Kotchi niwa korarehen de.*

1	平社員：	部長、明日おられますか？
2	部長：	おる思うけど、ちょっと調べてみるわ。
3		あっ、あかんわ、明日おらへんわ。なんで？
4	平社員：	あの，高木さん明日こっちに来るてゆうてはるんですけど。
5	部長：	えっ？明日、高木も同じ会議に出るんやで。
6		こっちには来られへんで。

1	EMPLOYEE:	Will you be in tomorrow, sir?
2	CHIEF:	I think so but let me check.
3		No, I'll be out tomorrow. Why do you ask?
4	EMPLOYEE:	Well, Mr. Takagi says he's coming here tomorrow.
5	CHIEF:	Huh? He's going to the same meeting as me.
6		He won't be here.

Line 1: As elsewhere in Japan, managers and other people with titles are often called by their job title instead of their name. In this case, the section chief is not called by his own name but *buchō* 部長. The passive form of *oru* is used to make the question more polite since the speaker's conversation partner is of a higher rank.

Line 4: *Yūteharun* ゆうてはるん is used to make the verb *yū* (*iu* 言う) more formal. In standard Japanese, he would have said *osshatte iru* おっしゃっている. From the employee's use of the formal form when referring to Takagi-*san,* we can assume that Takagi is either a customer, a higher level employee, or simply someone the employee is unfamiliar with.

Line 5: The boss does not speak politely to his employees. His sentences end with *de,* which is fairly rough (see 26). *Deru* 出る, in this case, means "to attend." We can also assume that Takagi is of roughly the same rank or lower than the section chief by the lack of honorific language used when referring to Takagi.

Conversation 4: Two college boys on the telephone.

1	TADASHI:	*Shige-yan?*
2	SHIGERU:	*Ā, hisashiburi ya na.*
3	TADASHI:	*Ima, nani shiten nen? Famikon?*
4	SHIGERU:	*Chau chau. Ima bideo miten nen.*
5	TADASHI:	*Sukebe na yatsu yaro.*
6	SHIGERU:	*Aho. Futsū no ya de.*

1	正：	しげやん？
2	茂：	ああ、久しぶりやな。
3	正：	今、何してんねん？ファミコン？
4	茂：	ちゃう、ちゃう。今ビデオ見てんねん。
5	正：	すけべなやつやろ。
6	茂：	アホ。普通のやで。

1	TADASHI:	Shige?
2	SHIGERU:	Hi. How have you been?
3	TADASHI:	What are you doing now? Video games?
4	SHIGERU:	No, I'm watching a movie now.
5	TADASHI:	I'll bet it's a dirty movie.
6	SHIGERU:	Don't be stupid. It's a regular one.

Line 1: In Kansai, *-yan* －やん is affixed to the names of friends. This is most commonly used among school-age boys, but older people also use it among very close friends.

Line 2: *Ya na* やな is equivalent to *da ne* だね in standard Japanese.

Line 3: *Shite irun da* is contracted to *shiten nen* してんねん. *Famikon* ファミコン, the Japanese word for Nintendo, Sega, and other home video games, is a contraction of "family computer."

Line 4: *Mite iru* 見ている in standard Japanese is *miten nen* 見てんねん in Kansai-*ben*.

Line 5: *Sukebe* すけべ, as well as *etchi* エッチ, means lewd or dirty-minded. *Sukebe* is properly written *sukebei* 助平, but is usually pronounced without the final *-i* sound. *Sukebe* is considered a more vulgar word than *etchi* and is therefore used infrequently by women, especially outside of Osaka. *Yaro* やろ is equivalent to *darō* だろう, the informal version of *deshō* でしょう in standard Japanese.

■ 3 ■
Kinki Variations
Kansai-*ben* Across Kansai

Throughout most of this book, we have concentrated on Kansai-*ben* as it is spoken in Osaka. Just as the Japanese language as a whole is slowly converging toward one standard due to the influence of the education system, national media, and movement of people, regional variations in Kansai-*ben* are slowly disappearing. Although the dialects spoken in such places as Osaka, Kyoto, and Mie were historically so different from each other as to be essentially incomprehensible to non-residents of the immediate area, the differences are now relatively minor, especially among young people. Variations remain, however, in pronunciation, level of politeness, and sentence endings. Within Kansai the difference between an individual's manner of speech due to personality, age, sex, and context of the conversation is now much greater than any difference due to one's place of birth.

We asked many people throughout Kinki if they could identify someone from their hometown by listening to that person's speech. Surprisingly, the answer, almost unanimously, was that it is impossible, especially among young people. Nevertheless, there are still some differences in people's speech that tend to characterize them as residents of certain areas. We've compiled a list of some of these characteristics, but many are traditional and not used that often now. We strongly recommend that you listen to your neighbors and colleagues to hear how they speak.

Osaka 大阪

Even within Osaka there have been traditional differences in the language spoken in various parts of the prefecture, especially between north and south. While these have virtually disappeared, there are still a few noticeable trends.

The southern half of the prefecture, especially Kawachi, has a reputation for the roughest, least polite speech in Kansai. The sentence ending *ke*, as in *ē yan ke* ええやんけ (That's fine!), has a very rough, rude sound and is heard more often here than elsewhere in Kansai. Only here would it be used by women as well as men. Another well-known example of Kawachi-*ben* is the use of the emphatic sentence ending *ware!* われ! which roughly translates to *da ne, kimi!* だね、君! in standard Japanese.

A few of the words that are considered traditional Kansai-*ben*, such as *erai kotcha* and *mōkarimakka*, are really Osaka-*ben,* and their usage is

essentially limited to inside Osaka. While it is difficult to generalize, it seems the usage of Kansai-*ben* is more prevalent in Osaka than in other Kansai cities, such as Kyoto and Kobe. This may be because Osaka-*jin* are proud of their heritage and less willing than those from smaller cities to accept Tokyo's mandates. On the other hand, it may be because Osaka-*jin* have a rougher way of speaking and therefore use standard Japanese (considered more polite) less often than residents of other cities in Kansai.

Nevertheless, nearly every salaryman and office lady in Osaka and throughout Kansai has learned to speak standard Japanese for use in business, although their pronunciation may differ slightly from Tokyoites. It is in the countryside of Kansai, among the grandmothers and grandfathers long isolated from the rest of Japan and without any need to ever speak to anyone from outside their village, where true Kansai-*ben* is preserved.

Kyoto 京都

The language in Kyoto is generally softer, more refined, and less direct than anywhere else in Japan. This may be because Kyoto was the capital of Japan for most of the country's history and its manner of politics required avoiding offending anyone who might either be important or likely to become important.

The most noticeable characteristic of Kyoto-*ben* is the high frequency usage of the *-haru* －はる form, which is considered *keigo* throughout the rest of Kansai. This form is used so frequently in Kyoto, even in informal situations, that it is not really considered as honorific here. It is used almost as frequently by men as by women in Kyoto, whereas it is used more often by women elsewhere. Because it is considered an honorific form, it is used to show respect to the conversation partner or to a third person. In Kyoto it is used only to add a touch of politeness to the conversation and can therefore be used when talking about a member of your own family, or even an animal. It is also often conjugated with the *-ta* －た verb stem in Kyoto, while it is usually attached to the *-te* －て or *-i* －い form of the verb in the rest of Kansai.

English:	What are you doing?
Kyoto:	*Nani shitaharu no?* 何したはるの？ (regular speech)
	Nani shitaharun desu ka? 何したはるんですか？ (regular or formal speech)
Osaka:	*Nani shiteharun desu ka?* 何してはるんですか？ (formal only)
	Nani shiteharu no? 何してはるの？ (regular or formal)
	Nani shiten nen? 何してんねん？ (informal)
Tokyo:	*Nani shiteru no?* 何してるの？ (informal)

Similarly, *-nahare* －なはれ is the imperative form and equivalent to *-nasai* －なさい in standard Japanese.

English:	Go to Kyoto!
Kyoto:	*Kyōto ni ikinahare.* 京都に行きなはれ。
Osaka:	*Kyōto iki.* 京都行き。
Tokyo:	*Kyōto ni ikinasai.* 京都に行きなさい。

In the same vein of over-politeness, Kyotoites use the honorific suffix -*san* even with inanimate objects, such as Daimaru-*san* 大丸さん to denote Daimaru Department Store.

Another characteristic that is not exclusive to Kyoto but more prevalent there than in other places in Kansai is the usage of *i* sounds in negative verbs instead of *e*.

KYOTO	KANSAI	TOKYO	ENGLISH
shiihin しいひん	*sēhen* せえへん	*shinai* しない	don't do
kiihin きいひん	*kēhen* けえへん	*konai* 来ない	don't come
dekihin できひん	*dekehen* でけへん	*dekinai* 出来ない	can't do

In actuality, both forms are used throughout Kansai and nowadays are based more on personal speech habits than on location, but the *i* form seems somewhat more prevalent in Kyoto, while the *e* form is more common elsewhere.

The pronunciation in Kyoto is softer and more melodic than elsewhere in Kansai. It is usually spoken slowly with clear pronunciation of what are usually silent vowels in Japanese, such as the *u* sound in -*masu*.

The usage of the sentence ending *nen* ねん is uncommon in Kyoto, while *nā* なあ is used frequently and usually drawn out for softness.

English:	My mother went to Kawaramachi yesterday.
Kyoto:	*Kinō nā, uchi no okāsan Kawaramachi ikahatte, nā.* きのうなあ、うちのお母さん河原町行かはって、なあ。
Osaka:	*Kinō na, uchi no okāsan Kawaramachi itten.* きのうな、うちのお母さん河原町行ってん。
Tokyo:	*Kinō ne, uchi no okāsan Kawaramachi ittan da.* きのうね、うちのお母さん河原町行ったんだ。

Probably the most difficult aspect of Kyoto-*ben* for foreigners to pick up, especially those familiar with Osaka-*ben*, is the dialect's lack of directness, as in the following example:

Mā, bubuzuke demo oagariyasu.
まあ、ぶぶづけでもおあがりやす。

This literally translates as "How about eating *ochazuke* (rice soup)?" but is actually an indirect way of telling guests they have overstayed their welcome. Kyoto residents, hearing this, would explain they were running much too late to partake of the host's hospitality and, in fact, would unfortunately have to be leaving immediately.

There are also many grammatical expressions and sentence endings that, while no longer used often by young people, seem to define traditional Kyoto-*ben*.

(a) -*yoshi*　－よし　　had better, please try

This is conjugated to the same verb stem as -*masu* verbs in standard Japanese.

English:	You should eat this.
Kyoto:	*Kore tabeyoshi.* これ食べよし。
Osaka:	*Kore tabena.* これ食べな。
Tokyo:	*Kore tabete.* これ食べて。

English: You should try eating this.
Kyoto: *Kore tabete miyoshi.* これ食べてみよし。
Osaka: *Kore tabete mii.* これ食べてみい。
Tokyo: *Kore tabete mite.* これ食べてみて。

English: You ought to go to Kyoto.
Kyoto: *Kyōto ikiyoshi.* 京都行きよし。
Osaka: *Kyōto ikana.* 京都行かな。
Tokyo: *Kyōto itte.* 京都行って。

(b) *e*   え   (sentence ending equivalent to *de* で in Osaka or *yo* よ in Tokyo)

English: I'm going to Kyoto!
Kyoto: *Kyōto iku e.* 京都行くえ。
Osaka: *Kyōto iku de.* 京都行くで。
Tokyo: *Kyōto iku yo.* 京都行くよ。

(c) *dosu*   どす   (Kyoto equivalent to *desu* in standard Japanese)

English: Kyoto is really beautiful.
Kyoto: *Kyōto honma ni kirei dosu nā.* 京都ほんまに奇麗どす なあ。
Osaka: *Kyōto honma ni kirei ya wa.* 京都ほんまに奇麗やわ。
Tokyo: *Kyōto hontō ni kirei da yo.* 京都本当に奇麗だよ。

Kobe 神戸

Kobe, although less than a thirty-minute train ride from Osaka station, has its own history and, of course, a slightly different dialect. The most identifiable aspect of Kobe-*ben* is the use of the verb conjugation -*tō* -とう and -*ton* -とん, rather than -*ten nen*, to create the -ing form of verbs.

English: What are you doing now?
Kobe: *Ima, nani shiton?* 今、何しとん？
Osaka: *Ima, nani shiten nen?* 今、何してんねん？
Tokyo: *Ima, nani shiteru?* 今、何してる？

English: I'm studying now.
Kobe: *Ima benkyō shitō.* 今、勉強しとう。
Osaka: *Ima benkyō shiten nen.* 今、勉強してんねん。
Tokyo: *Ima benkyō shiteru.* 今、勉強してる。

There is also less use of *na* and *nā* in Kobe than in Osaka. Women in Kobe also use *ne* more often.

Characteristics of Other Areas of Kansai

The language in areas outside the Kei-Han-Shin triangle is also becoming a mixture of the old ways of speaking, the style of the nearest cities, and, to some extent, standard Japanese. The older generation, of course, sticks to their local dialect while younger people, influenced by television, education, and travel, are adopting more standard Japanese into their speech. It is nearly impossible to generalize how people speak in each place, but there are a few patterns that are common in certain regions of Kansai that are not part of regular Kansai-*ben*.

In Wakayama and rural parts of Nara Prefecture, *z* sounds are replaced by *d* sounds. For example, instead of saying *zen-zen* 全然, people in this area say *den-den* デンデン. In the Shiga area, *yaharu* やはる replaces -*haru* 一はる. People in Himeji say *otteya* おってや instead of *iteharu* いてはる. There are, of course, many such variations across the Kinki region, and it is impossible to describe them all here, but we have listed a few of the more interesting words you might hear if you travel across the area.

DIALECT	LOCATION	STANDARD KANSAI-*BEN*	ENGLISH
akanasho あかなしょ	Wakayama	*akan* あかん	no good
den-den でんでん	Wakayama	*zen-zen* 全然	not at all
dero デロ	Wakayama	*zero* ゼロ	zero
dontsuki どんつき	Nara	*tsukiatari* 突き当たり	end of street/corridor
gō ga waku 剛が沸く	Himeji	*hara ga tatsu* 腹が立つ	angry
mominai もみない	Nara	*shōmonai* しょうもない	trifling
otoroshii おとろしい	Nara	*mendōkusai* 面倒臭い	pain in the neck
otteya おってや	Himeji	*iteharu* いてはる	honorific for *iru*
shiyaharu しやはる	Shiga	*shiharu* しはる	honorific for *suru*
tekyara てきゃら	Wakayama	*aitsura* あいつら	those guys
waera わえら	Wakayama	*orera* 俺ら	us

▪ 4 ▪

Fifteen More Words
Needed To Survive

Now that you have mastered the first fifteen absolutely crucial words, and realized how useful speaking Kansai-*ben* is to survival here, let's move on to the next fifteen. It is nearly impossible to construct a sample conversation without using at least a few of these words.

VOCABULARY

16. *bochi-bochi* ぽちぽち
17. *gottsui* ごっつい
18. *hona, honnara, sonnara* ほな、ほんなら、そんなら
19. *mōkarimakka* もうかりまっか
20. *omoroi* おもろい
21. *shindoi* しんどい
22. *suki ya nā* 好きやなあ
23. *uttōshii* 鬱陶しい
24. *yō* よう
25. *yū* ゆう（言う）

GRAMMATICAL EXPRESSIONS

26. *de* で
27. *-han* ーはん
28. *na, nā* な、なあ
29. *-san* ーさん
30. *wa* わ

16. *bochi-bochi (denna)*   ぽちぽち (でんな)   so-so, not bad, no problems, fine

Bochi-bochi has a wide variety of vague meanings, such as "so-so" or "slowly improving." Its most stereotypical usage is as the proper response to *mōkarimakka?* (See 19) Usually, *denna* でんな, a contracted form of *desu ne* ですね, is attached to the end. *Mā* まあ is often inserted at the beginning.

SUMIYOSHI:	*Mōkarimakka?*
SAKAI:	*Mā, bochi-bochi denna.*
住吉：	もうかりまっか？
堺：	まあ、ぽちぽちでんな。
SUMIYOSHI:	How's business?
SAKAI:	So-so.

   However, unlike *mōkarimakka, bochi-bochi* is still used quite frequently in Kansai. It can be an effective neutral response to any embarrassing question you do not wish to answer.

HIRAKATA:	*Ima no shigoto, susunden no?*
IBARAGI:	*Mā, bochi-bochi ya na.*
枚方：	今の仕事、進んでの？
茨木：	まあ、ぽちぽちやな。
HIRAKATA:	How's the project progressing?
IBARAGI:	Moving along slowly.

HORIUCHI:	*Kansai-ben, mō nareta?*
PALTER:	*Mā, bochi-bochi ya na.*
堀内：	関西弁、もう慣れた？
ポーター：	まあ、ぽちぽちやな。

HORIUCHI: Have you gotten used to the Kansai dialect yet?

PALTER: Getting there.

Bochi-bochi is also used as a synonym for the standard Japanese *soro-soro* そろそろ, meaning "It is time."

Bochi-bochi iko ka.
ぼちぼち行こか。
It's time to go now.

Bochi-bochi is always a good response whenever someone asks you the inevitable "Can you speak Japanese?" or (even after you have lived in Japan for thirty years) "Can you use chopsticks?" This response will show that you not only speak Japanese but Kansai-*ben* as well! No matter where you live in Japan (or even overseas), this response is certain to provoke a laugh and start a conversation about Kansai or the Hanshin Tigers.

TAKESHITA: *Kyan yū supiiku Japaniizu?*

PALTER: *Mā, bochi-bochi ya na.*

TAKESHITA: *Eh? Kettai na gaijin ya nā.*

竹下： キャン ユウ スピーク ジャパニーズ？

ポーター： まあ、ぽちぽちやな。

竹下： えっ？ けったいな外人やなあ。

TAKESHITA: Can you speak Japanese?

PALTER: Sure!

TAKESHITA: Huh? What a strange foreigner.

Kettai けったい is equivalent to *hen* 変 or *myō* 妙 . Like these synonyms, *kettai* carries negative connotations meaning "strange" or "perverted." The meaning depends on the context, and can also have positive connotations, such as "interesting" or "different." It is difficult to determine which meaning is implied here, but we hope the foreigner who can speak Kansai-*ben* is considered to be more interesting than perverted.

17. *gottsui*   ごっつい   very, big

Gottsui usually means "very" and is similar in usage to *metcha* めっちゃ and *mutcha* むっちゃ. While *gottsui* is the traditional Osaka word, *metcha* and *mutcha* now seem to be preferred by young people, especially those living outside the city, although *gottsui* is still used to describe extreme conditions. With its very course sound, women use *gottsui* only to express very strong emphasis, preferring *metcha* or *mutcha* for normal situations. As with other Kansai-*ben* adjectives, it is common for the final *i* sound to be dropped and the *u* sound extended, in this case producing *gottsu*—.

Gottsui ē nā .
ごっついええなあ。
Really good.

Gottsū shigoto aru wa.
ごっつう仕事あるわ。
I've got a lot of work to do.

Aitsu, gottsui nā.
あいつ、ごっついなあ。
He's really big.

Gottsui kii.
ごっつい木い。
A huge tree.

18. ***hona, honnara, sonnara***　　ほな、ほんなら、そんなら　　in that case,
if so, then

All three of these words have the same meaning of "if that is true,
then . . ." All are contracted forms of *sore nara* それなら. In general,
hona is used more often by women and *honnara* by men. *Hona* and
honnara can also mean "see you later." (See 61)

SUMIYOSHI:	*Sore, nanbo?*
SAKAI:	*Hyaku rokujū en ya.*
SUMIYOSHI:	*Honnara, kau wa.*
住吉：	それ、なんぼ？
堺：	百六十円や。
住吉：	ほんなら、買うわ。
SUMIYOSHI:	How much is that?
SAKAI:	It's 160 yen.
SUMIYOSHI:	In that case, I'll take it.

HIKARI:	*Nā, nā, nani shiten no?*
NOZOMI:	*Gomen. Ima, isogashii nen.*
HIKARI:	*Hona, ē wa. Mata kuru wa.*

光： なあ、なあ、何してんの？
望： ご免。今、忙しいねん。
光： ほな、ええわ。また来るわ。

HIKARI: Hey, what are you up to?

NOZOMI: Sorry, I'm kind of busy now.

HIKARI: Well, no problem. I'll come back later.

19. *mōkarimakka*   もうかりまっか   How are you? How's business?
Mōkarimakka is another typical Kansai word that everyone across Japan thinks Kansai-ites use regularly but, in fact, is rarely used nowadays. When used, it is as a greeting, especially to a shopkeeper whose store you regularly patronize. The pronunciation *mōkattemakka* もうかってまっか is also sometimes heard.

Mōkarimakka is derived from *mōkaru* 儲かる, which means to make a profit. The fact that this was once the typical greeting, even to those essentially unconcerned with money (just as Americans might say "how's business?" even to students or other nonbusiness-related people), is used as ammunition by outsiders who look down on Osaka as a city of merchants.

To be honest, we have never heard *mōkarimakka* used in conversation except as a joke. However, because it is always mentioned as a well-known example of Osaka-*ben*, as a foreigner speaking Kansai-*ben*, you will be expected to know and to be able to use this word. See word entry 16 for the proper response if anyone ever asks you *mōkarimakka*?

20. *omoroi*   おもろい   interesting
Omoroi is a contraction of the standard Japanese word *omoshiroi* 面白い. It can be conjugated in the same manner as other adjectives, although the *ku* syllable is usually dropped in the negative conjugation.

omorokatta   おもろかった   was interesting

omoronai	おもろない	not interesting
omoronakatta	おもろなかった	wasn't interesting

As with other adjectives, *omoroi* can be attached to nouns.

omoroi yatcha	おもろいやっちゃ	interesting person
omoronai bangumi	おもろない番組	uninteresting show

SHIGERU:	*Kono eiga, omorokatta nā.*
TADASHI:	*Honma? Zen-zen omoronakatta omo kedo nā.*
茂：	この映画、おもろかったなあ。
正：	ほんま？ 全然おもろなかったおもけどなあ。
SHIGERU:	This movie was interesting, don't you think?
TADASHI:	Really? I thought it was completely uninteresting.

Omo おも is the shortened form of *omou* 思う.

21. *shindoi*　しんどい　tired, tiring, difficult

Shindoi is an all-purpose word used to express being tired or to indicate that something is tiring or difficult. It is probably the most often used word in the office and at the health club, and can also mean being somewhat under the weather. It is conjugated the same way as other adjectives.

Konna shigoto, shindoi wa.
こんな仕事、しんどいわ。
This type of work is tough.

Kyō, shindokatta wa.
今日、しんどかったわ。
I had a rough day today.

Erai えらい (see word entry 46) also means tiring, but is not used nearly as widely as *shindoi*.

22. *suki ya nā*　　好きやなあ　　like

This is no different from the standard *suki* 好き, but we include it here because of the frequency with which it is heard in this form, and because of the difference in pronunciation. In standard Japanese, *suki* 好き is pronounced with a nearly silent *u,* as in "ski." In Kansai, the *u* is fully pronounced and the first syllable is accented, *SU-ki.* This is usually followed by *ya nā* やなあ or *ya ne* やね .

Suki ya nā can refer to things and people liked by other people as well as to your own personal preferences.

At an *oden* stand:

SUZUKI:	*Kanto-daki honma ni suki ya nā.*
HONDA:	*So ya nen. Metcha suki ya nen. Toku ni kono mise no ga umain ya.*
鈴木：	関東煮、ほんまに好きやなあ。
本田：	そやねん。めっちゃ好きやねん。特にこの店のが旨いんや。
SUZUKI:	You really like *Kanto-daki*, don't you.
HONDA:	Yup. I love it. And this stand is especially good.

Kanto-daki 関東煮 is the Kansai word for what is called *oden* おでん in Tokyo.

At a karaoke box:

MIKA:	*Kono uta suki ya nā.*
TOMOKO:	*Itsumo kore ya nen.*
美香：	この歌好きやなあ。
友子：	いつもこれやねん。

MIKA: You really like this song, huh?

TOMOKO: I always sing this one.

23. *uttōshii*   鬱陶しい   gloomy, dreary

(especially in reference to the weather)

Although part of standard Japanese, *uttōshii* is heard much more often in Kansai, not because the weather is worse in Kansai (it's actually slightly better than Tokyo, although it still gets its full share of *uttōshii* weather) but simply as a matter of word choice. Tokyoites usually say *iya na tenki* いやな天気 instead. In Kansai, *uttōshii* is also used to describe persistent, slimy people.

Kyō, uttōshii nā .
今日、鬱陶しいなあ。
It's pretty ugly out today.

Uttōshii yatcha nā .
鬱陶しいやっちゃなあ。
That guy is really slimy!

Yatcha やっちゃ is a contraction of *yatsu ya* 奴や, meaning a person or thing.

24. yō   よう   very, much, often, well

Yō is a contraction of *yoku* よく, the adverb form of *yoi* 良い , meaning "good."

Yō kutta.
よう食った。
I ate a lot.

Yō wakattoru.
よう分かっとる。
I completely understand.

Yō sēhen wa.
ようせえへんわ。
I can't do this well.

25. yū   ゆう（言う）   to speak

The verb *iu* 言う in Kansai is usually pronounced *yū* ゆう. While in this dictionary form it is difficult to hear the difference in pronunciation, the conjugated forms are easily distinguishable.

yūta (instead of *itta*)	ゆうた (いった)	said
yūten (*itta*)	ゆうてん (いった)	said
yūteru (*itteru*)	ゆうてる (いってる)	saying
yūtotten (*itteta*)	ゆうとってん (いってた)	was saying

Nani yūten nen?
何ゆうてんねん？
What the hell are you saying?

Sono koto, anoko ni yūtoite.
その事、あの子にゆうといて。
Please tell that to her.

Mō ippen yūte kureru?
もう一遍ゆうてくれる?
Would you say that again?

26. *de* で (exclamatory sentence-ending particle)

De, unlike *na* (see 28), is used only at the end of sentences. Its meaning is somewhat like an exclamation point, strengthening the effect of the sentence. It is usually used when informing someone of something, but has a rough tone. In these respects, it is similar to *zo* in standard Japanese, but is used frequently by women as well as men.

tsuita de	着いたで	We've arrived!
atsui de	暑いで	It's hot!
ē de	ええで	This is fine!
iku de	行くで	I'm leaving! / Let's go!

27. *-han* －はん Mr., Mrs., Ms., Miss

-San, the standard honorific suffix attached to people's names, is altered in pronunciation in Kansai and becomes *-han*. This practice tends to be more common inside Osaka and among older people. It is not heard that often outside of Osaka.

Miyazawa-han	宮沢はん	Mr. Miyazawa
yome-han	嫁はん	wife
obā-han	おばあはん	old lady
anta-han	あんたはん	you

28. *na, nā* な、なあ (sentence-ending particles) don't you think? y'know?

It is nearly impossible to translate these sentence endings into English. The closest equivalent to *na* and *nā* is the habit of some young people to say "y'know?" or "eh?" at the end of sentences. Japanese will include some sort of word with no meaning at the end of every sentence, often in the middle of sentences, sometimes after nearly every word, and occasionally replacing the entire sentence. Sometimes these particle endings seem to have little meaning except to indicate the fact that the speaker is pausing for an instant. In Tokyo, the two main phrases are *ne* and *sa*. In Kansai, *na* is the preferred word. *Ne* is sometimes used in Kansai, especially by women, but *sa* is never used. In Tokyo, *na* is occasionally used, but it has a rough sound there, which is another reason that Kansai-*ben* sounds crude to untrained ears.

Just as *ne* is often lengthened to *nē*, *na* is very often lengthened to *nā*, especially when used at the end of sentences or when asking for some sort of response from the conversation partner.

TADASHI:	*Kore, na, wakarehen, nā.*
SHIGERU:	*Na!*
正 :	これ、な、分かれへん、なあ。
茂 :	なっ!
TADASHI:	This is, y'know, completely incomprehensible, isn't it?
SHIGERU:	Completely!

Like *ne, na* can be used by itself to indicate complete agreement with the speaker's opinion. It is not a soft *na*, but spoken with a short, strong expulsion of air. A drawn out *nā* can also be similarly used in Kansai.

Be careful not to confuse this sentence-ending *na* with the standard Japanese particle *na*, which is used with verbs to create the "must" or "must not" forms in such phrases as *benkyō suru na* 勉強するな (don't study) or *benkyō sena akan* 勉強せなあかん (have to study). In general, the grammatical partical *na* has a shorter sound and is used only in conjunction with verbs, but it can sometimes be difficult to tell which is intended except in the context of the conversation.

29. *-san*   —さん   (greetings suffix)

-San is added to the end of greetings such as "good morning." This is essentially the same *-san* that is used as a suffix to peoples' names, a contraction of the more formal *-sama* 様. The practice of attaching *-san* to greetings is a well-known aspect of the Kansai dialect, but is heard more often in Osaka. Because it is much less formal than standard greetings, it is used mostly with friends or co-workers of the same age or lower. This suffix cannot be applied to all greetings and, as a rule of thumb, can only be used with greetings that would normally end in *gozaimasu, gozaimashita,* or *sama.*

ohayō-san	お早うさん	good morning
omedetō-san	おめでとうさん	congratulations
arigatō-san	ありがとうさん	thanks
gokurō-san	ご苦労さん	thanks for your help

30. wa   わ   (untranslatable neutral sentence ending)

Wa is yet another Kansai-*ben* sentence ending. It has neutral connotations and is used for adding a slight amount of emphasis to the sentence. Unlike in Tokyo, where *wa* is a very soft sentence ending used exclusively by women, in Kansai *wa* is neutral and is used frequently by men as well. It is sometimes written as *wā* わあ to differentiate between the *wa* わ used by everyone in Kansai and the Tokyo *wa* わ used only by women. Still, in order to avoid silly comments about learning Japanese from girlfriends, it is probably best for male foreigners to avoid using *wa* until everyone has realized he is speaking Kansai-*ben*.

Mō ē wa.
もうええわ。
It's good enough. / I give up.

Shiran wa.
知らんわ。
I don't know.

Tanomu wa.
頼むわ。
Please.

    Wa is almost always used after *tanomu* 頼む when saying "please" or "I'm counting on you." (See 38) Because *wa* is a polite way to add emphasis to a sentence, it is often heard with somewhat formal language. *Desu* + *wa* and *-masu* + *wa* are very common sentence patterns in Kansai.

Ii desu wa.
いいですわ。
I don't mind. / No thanks. (formal)

Ē desu wa.
ええですわ。
I don't mind. / No thanks. (slightly less formal)

Orimasu wa.
おりますわ。
I'm here.

▪ 5 ▪

Example Conversations II

Conversation 1: Two old merchants.

1	HANAKO:	*Ohayō-san. Ojii-han, karada no chōshi donai?*
2	ICHITARŌ:	*Mā, bochi-bochi ya na.*
3	HANAKO:	*Sonnara, issho ni Yoshimoto mi ni ikahen?*
4	ICHITARŌ:	*Omoroin ka?*
5	HANAKO:	*Gottsui ninki ya de.*
6	ICHITARŌ:	*Sonnan yūte mo nā,*
7		*Minami iku no chotto shindoi wa.*

1	花子：	お早うさん。おじいはん、体の調子どない？
2	一太郎：	まあ、ぼちぼちやな。
3	花子：	そんなら、一緒に吉本見に行かへん？
4	一太郎：	おもろいんか？
5	花子：	ごっつい人気やで。
6	一太郎：	そんなんゆうてもなあ、
7		ミナミ行くのちょっとしんどいわ。

69

1	HANAKO:	Good morning. How are you feeling?
2	ICHITARŌ:	Not bad.
3	HANAKO:	In that case, let's go see Yoshimoto.
4	ICHITARŌ:	Is it interesting?
5	HANAKO:	It's really popular.
6	ICHITARŌ:	That may be true, but
7		it's a bit of a pain to go all the way to Nanba.

Line 1: *Ojii-han* means Mr. Old Man or Grandpa, but does not carry the negative connotations it would have in English and is often preferred over the use of actual names. *Donai* is equivalent to *dō* どう, in this case meaning "How is it?"

Line 3: Osaka is very famous for its sense of humor, and one popular form of comedy is *manzai*, or stand-up comedy teams. Yoshimoto is short for Yoshimoto Kōgyō 吉本興業, a vaudeville and comedy entertainment agency based in Nanba that has spawned a whole generation of comedians who have become famous throughout Japan, even in humorless Tokyo! They operate two theaters in Nanba, Nanba Kagetsu and Nichōme Gekijō. Watching a live performance of young Yoshimoto talent may help you learn Kansai-*ben* and understand Kansai humor, but it isn't necessary to travel all the way to Nanba to see them. They also produce a popular television show called "Yoshimoto Shinkigeki." Each actor has a stock of funny phrases which he uses each week, and these soon make their way into the speech of young people in Kansai. Thanks to Yoshimoto, the vast majority of comedians in Japan are from Kansai and have helped popularize Kansai-*ben* throughout Japan. Because of this agency, people living outside of Kansai tend to believe that everyone in Kansai is a comedian. Due to the use of Kansai-*ben* in comedy, even when Kansai people are discussing serious matters, it sounds like comedy to everyone else. Actually, the percentage of people who think that making others laugh is their life's work may be very high in Kansai.

One of the basic patterns of *manzai* comedy is *boke* ボケ and *tsukkomi* ツッコミ. *Boke* refers to the person playing the idiot while *tsukkomi* is the straight man in a two-man comedy team. The role of the *boke* is to say something strange or stupid. When he does, the *tsukkomi* has to throw in the proper straight line to make people laugh. This pattern is also common in everyday conversations in Osaka. When someone says something strange, stupid, or silly, reminiscent of the *boke* role, other people are expected to add the *tsukkomi* line.

The easiest and most common of these *tsukkomi* phrases are as follows:

Nna aho na!
んなアホな！
That's really stupid!

Nande ya nen?
何でやねん？
Gee, I wonder why?

Anta to wa yattoren wa.
あんたとはやっとれんわ。
I should quit being your partner.

Hona, sainara.
ほな、さいなら。
In that case, I'm out of here.

Chan-chan.
ちゃんちゃん。
It's all over.

Line 7: The Nanba area, on the southern end of downtown Osaka, is called Minami ミナミ by Osaka residents, and Kita キタ refers to Umeda, one of the main districts of Osaka on the northern end of the loop line. It includes the main train stations for JR (Osaka Station) and Hankyū and Hanshin (Umeda Station), as well as a large business and entertainment district. Although these names obviously refer to the old north and south ends of Osaka, Minami and Kita are always written in katakana and never kanji.

Conversation 2: Between two high school students.

1	KAZUO:	*Ore, omae no koto suki ya nen.*
2	MARI:	*Honma?*
3		*Sonnan jōdan, chaun?*
4		*Itsumo "kirai ya" yūteru yan.*
5	KAZUO:	*Aho ya nā.*
6		*Ore, tereya yakara,*
7		*honma no kimochi, iwarehenkatten.*

1	一雄：	俺、お前の事好きやねん。
2	真理：	ほんま？
3		そんなん冗談ちゃうん？
4		いつも「嫌いや」ゆうてるやん。
5	一雄：	アホやなあ。
6		俺、照れややから、
7		ほんまの気持ち、言われへんかってん。

1	KAZUO:	I really like you.
2	MARI:	You're lying.
3		You're just joking, right?
4		You always say you hate me.
5	KAZUO:	Don't be stupid.
6		I'm shy so,
7		I could never say what I really felt.

Line 1: *Anta/Omae no koto ga suki* is the usual way to tell someone you like them in the romantic sense. Its meaning is somewhere between

"I like you" and "I love you." *Omae* お前 means the same as *anata,* but is rougher sounding and used exclusively by males.

Line 6: *Tereya* is a person who tends to be *tereru* 照れる, which means to be shy or easily embarrassed.

Line 7: *Kimochi* 気持ち means feelings.

Conversation 3: Two male college students.

1	SHIGERU:	*Eiga mi ni ikehen?*
2	TADASHI:	*Omae, eiga honma ni suki ya nā.*
3	SHIGERU:	*Se yaro.*
4		*Ima gottsui omoroi eiga yatten nen de.*
5	TADASHI:	*Eh? Honma kainā.*
6		*Mae mo sō yūteta kedo,*
7		*zen-zen omoronakatta yan ka.*
8	SHIGERU:	*Nani yūten nen, omae.*
9		*Sore omae ga eranda yatsu yan ka.*
10	TADASHI:	*Mō yō oboetehen na.*
11	SHIGERU:	*Honnara, kondo wa ore erabu wa na.*
12		*Ashita san-ji ni iko ka?*

1	茂：	映画見に行けへん？
2	正：	お前、映画ほんまに好きやなあ。
3	茂：	せやろ。
4		今ごっつぃおもろい映画やってんねんで。
5	正：	えっ？ほんまかいなあ。
6		前もそうゆうてたけど、
7		全然おもろなかったやんか。
8	茂：	何ゆうてんねん、お前。
9		それお前が選んだやつやんか。

10 正：　　　　もうよう覚えてへんな。

11 茂：　　　　ほんなら、今度は俺選ぶわな。

12　　　　　　明日、3時に行こか？

1	SHIGERU:	Do you wanna go see a movie?
2	TADASHI:	You really like movies, don't you?
3	SHIGERU:	You'd better believe it!
4		There's a really good movie playing now.
5	TADASHI:	Huh? Don't be stupid.
6		Last time you said that,
7		the movie was awful.
8	SHIGERU:	What the hell are you saying?
9		You picked that one!
10	TADASHI:	Maybe. I don't remember well.
11	SHIGERU:	Well, I'm picking this one.
12		Let's go at 3:00 tomorrow.

Line 3: *Se* せ is a Kansai version of *sō* そう. It is almost always followed by *ya* や or *yaro* やろ.

Line 4: *De* で is used after *nen* in this case to strengthen the sentence. It has a slightly rough tone that is to be expected in a conversation between close friends.

Line 5: *Honma kainā* ほんまかいなあ is a very sarcastic way to say "really?" (See 41)

Line 6: *Yūteta* ゆうてた replaces *itteta* 言ってた, meaning "was saying." *Omoroi* is conjugated in the negative past tense to *omoronakatta*, "wasn't interesting."

Line 8: *Nani* + [*-ten nen* form of verb], *omae* is a very common male speech pattern in Kansai when asking a rhetorical question.

Nani yūten nen, omae?
何ゆうてんねん、お前？
What are you saying?

Nani yatten nen, omae?
何やってんねん、お前？
What are you doing?

Line 9: *Yatsu* 奴 in this case means "thing" instead of the usual meaning of "person."

Line 10: *Yō oboetehen* よう覚えてへん is the contracted form of *yoku oboete inai* よく覚えていない, or "don't remember well." *Yō* before a negative verb is a very common pattern.

Yō sēhen.
ようせえへん。
Don't do well.

Yō miehen.
よう見えへん。
Can't see well.

Yō wakaran.
よう分からん。
Don't know.

Conversation 4: Between Sakai, a shopkeeper, and Sumiyoshi, an acquaintance.

1 SUMIYOSHI: *Ohayō-san, Sakai-han. Mōkarimakka?*

2 SAKAI: *Mā, bochi-bochi denna.*
3   *Kyō, uttōshii nā.*
4 SUMIYOSHI: *So ya nā. Ima nimo furisō ya nā. Mushiatsui shi.*
5   *Nanka mō shindoi wa. Shigoto shita nai wa.*
6 SAKAI: *Mā, sonna koto iwanto*
7   *bochi-bochi yarimahyo.*

1 住吉： お早うさん、堺はん。もうかりまっか？
2 堺：   まあ、ぼちぼちでんな。
3   今日、鬱陶しいなあ。
4 住吉： そやなあ。今にも降りそうやなあ。蒸し暑いし。
5   なんかもうしんどいわ。仕事したないわ。
6 堺：   まあ、そんな事いわんと
7   ぼちぼちやりまひょ。

1 SUMIYOSHI: Good morning, Mr. Sakai. How're things?
2 SAKAI: Not bad, not bad.
3   It's pretty ugly out today, eh?

4	SUMIYOSHI:	Yeah. It looks like it's going to rain. And it's hot and humid.
5		I'm already tired of working. I don't want to keep working.
6	SAKAI:	Don't say that,
7		let's just work at our own pace.

Line 1: *Ohayō-san* replaces *ohayō gozaimasu* when saying "good morning" to friends or neighbors. *Sakai-han* is used in place of *Sakai-san*, but is less formal. Among males, even good friends call each other by last names, but in this case the two are not close enough to dispense with the honorific titles. They are probably too old to use *-kun* and not close enough to use *-yan*.

Line 5: In this case, *mō shindoi* もうしんどい probably means not that he's tired from working but that he doesn't feel like working in the hot and humid weather. *Shita nai wa* したないわ is equivalent to *shitakunai* したくない meaning "don't want to," in this case referring to work. The *ku* sound is often left out.

Line 7: As opposed to line 2, this time *bochi-bochi* ぼちぼち means "take our time." *Yarimahyo* やりまひょ is equivalent to *yarimashō* やりましょう. "S" sounds are often changed to "h" sounds in Kansai, especially by older people in Osaka. Similarly, *-masen* verb endings are often changed to *-mahen,* and *-mashō* to *-mahyo*.

▪ 6 ▪
Tora-Kichi

Living in Kansai is synonymous with rooting for the Hanshin Tigers baseball team. Even people who hate baseball will say they hope Hanshin wins. There are two other teams in Kansai, the Orix BlueWave in Kobe and the Kintetsu Buffaloes of Osaka Prefecture, but they do not command nearly as much support or attention as Hanshin. This is not to say that Hanshin is a good team; in fact, since they were formed in 1935, they have only once won the Nihon Series, Japan's national championship. Most years find them languishing in the cellar of the Central League, which only seems to increase their lovability as the underdog. So don't be surprised when, even at the end of a formal company banquet, the corporate vice-president asks everyone to stand up and sing the Hanshin Tigers Fight Song, *Rokkō Oroshi*.

Memorizing the words to *Rokkō Oroshi*, accurately called *Hanshin Taigāsu no Uta* 阪神タイガースの歌, is a sure way to become popular in Kansai (and hated in Tokyo). Most karaoke clubs in the area have the song on their menu, and everyone in the place will surely join in singing it, especially near the end of the summer.

Rokkō is, of course, the Rokkō Mountains, and *Rokkō Oroshi* is the wind that blows down from Mt. Rokkō. The Tigers's home stadium is Kōshien in Nishinomiya, between Osaka and Kobe and near the base of Mt. Rokkō.

Rokkō Oroshi　六甲颪

Rokkō oroshi ni sassō to	六甲颪に颯爽と
Sōten kakeru nichirin no	蒼天翔ける日輪の
Seishun no haki uruwashiku	青春の覇気美しく
Kagayaku wagana zo Hanshin Taigāsu	輝く我が名ぞ阪神タイガース
Ō-ō-ō-ō Hanshin Taigāsu	オウオウオウオウ阪神タイガース
Fure-fure-fure-fure	フレフレフレフレ
Tōshi hatsuratsu tatsu ya ima	闘志溌剌起つや今
Nekketsu sude ni teki o tsuku	熱血既に敵を衝く
Jū-ō no iki takaraka ni	獣王の意気高らかに
Muteki no warera zo Hanshin Taigāsu	無敵の我等ぞ阪神タイガース
Ō-ō-ō-ō Hanshin Taigāsu	オウオウオウオウ阪神タイガース
Fure-fure-fure-fure	フレフレフレフレ
Tetsuwan kyōda ikuchi tabi	鉄腕強打幾千度び
Kitaete koko ni Kōshien	鍛えてここに甲子園
Shōri ni moyuru eikan wa	勝利に燃ゆる栄冠は
Kagayaku warera zo Hanshin Taigāsu	輝く我等ぞ阪神タイガース
Ō-ō-ō-ō Hanshin Taigāsu	オウオウオウオウ阪神タイガース
Fure-fure-fure-fure	フレフレフレフレ

Lyrics: Satō Sōnosuke	作詩：佐藤惣之助
Melody: Koseki Yūji	作曲：古関裕而

Rokkō Wind

In the Rokkō wind, a gallant
Orb galloping across the blue sky
A young, beautiful spirit
We are the sparkling Hanshin Tigers.
O— Hanshin Tigers
Hurray, hurray, hurray, hurray!

A fighting spirit awake,
Already beat back the enemy
With the pride of the king of animals
We are the invincible Hanshin Tigers.

Steel arms and powerful hitting, thousands of times
We are training here in Kōshien
Burning for the crown of victory
We are the sparkling Hanshin Tigers.

   Some useful words and phrases related to the Tigers are listed below.

dametora   駄目虎
When the Tigers are playing poorly and falling behind in the standings, they are called *dametora*, but only by non-Kansai residents. Hanshin fans, no matter how bad the season might seem, never give up on their Tigers.

dentō no issen   伝統の一戦
This is the name for the games between the Tigers and Kyojin 巨人 (Yomiuri Giants). The rivalry between the two teams is almost as intense as the rivalry between the two cities. The Giants are, of course, Tokyo's

main team. When the game between the two teams is played at Kōshien, it is called the Hanshin-Kyojin game. The home team's name comes first, so when the game is played at the Big Egg (Tokyo Dome) the order is reversed.

Hanshin   阪神
(a) Hanshin Tigers baseball team
(b) Hanshin Railway
(c) Companies owned by Hanshin Railway such as Hanshin Department Store
(d) The Osaka-Kobe region
(e) Hanshin horse racing track in Takarazuka

It is important to realize that baseball teams in Japan are named after the company that owns them, in this case Hanshin Railway. The characters for Hanshin 阪神 are an abbreviation of Osaka-Kobe 大阪ー神戸, and are used when referring to the two-city region. The railroad company that built a line connecting Kobe and Osaka was therefore named Hanshin Dentetsu 阪神電鉄 and, like most other major rail companies in Japan, has become a transportation and retailing conglomerate. If Hanshin wins

the pennant, look for bargain sales at Hanshin Hyakkaten 阪神百貨店, their department store.

jetto fūsen　ジェット風船
These are the long balloons that Tigers fans, especially those in the bleachers, release at the start of the bottom of the seventh inning. They are also referred to as *roketto fūsen* ロケット風船. The balloons make a whistling noise as they fly and create an amazing racket when everyone releases them at the same time.

Kōshien　甲子園
(a)　Baseball stadium in Nishinomiya where the Tigers play.
(b)　Twice annual high school baseball tournament held at Kōshien Stadium.
(c)　Stop on the Hanshin Railway line where Kōshien Stadium is located.

mōko　猛虎
Fierce Tigers. This is what they are called when they are playing well.

Rokkō　六甲
Mt. Rokkō, one peak of the Rokkō mountain range, which rises up behind Kōshien.

Rokkō Oroshi　六甲颪
The Hanshin Tigers team anthem, named after the first line of the song describing the wind blowing down Mt. Rokkō.

rakkii sebun　ラッキー7
Lucky 7, the seventh inning. Tradition says this is the strongest at-bat for the Tigers, when they often score runs to come from behind. When

Hanshin plays at home, the stadium makes an announcement over the loudspeakers in the middle of the inning to remind everyone to cheer even harder during Lucky 7.

shi no rōdo   死のロード

These are the so-called "deadly" road games. For two weeks in August, while the high school baseball tournament occupies Kōshien Stadium, the Tigers play only road games. This is a critical juncture in the season, and the team typically doesn't do well during this period.

Taigāsu fan   タイガースファン

A Tigers fan.

tora   虎

(a) The Japanese word for tiger.

(b) The Hanshin Tigers.

tora-kichi   虎キチ

Someone crazy about the Tigers, or a Tigers fan. The word is derived from *tora*, meaning tiger, and *kichi*, which is short for something we aren't allowed to print, meaning crazy or insane.

torakki トラッキ
The Tigers's mascot.

wakatora 若虎
A promising young Tigers player.

A trip to Kōshien to see a game is well worth the effort if tickets are available. Plan ahead—when the team is playing well, Hanshin tickets can be as difficult to come by as sumo wrestling tickets. But stay far away from the bleachers unless you're carrying something far stronger than aspirin. Although noisy throughout the stadium, the bleachers beyond the outfield are the epicenter of the non-stop orchestrated cheering. The Hanshin colors, yellow and black, or white and black, are essentially mandatory there.

It is also a smart idea to watch a few games on television, pick out a few favorite players, and keep track of the team's record and standings in the newspaper in order to have an easy topic of conversation with which to break the ice at parties and company functions.

One interesting piece of Tiger history involves a foreigner, Colonel

Sanders of Kentucky Fried Chicken fame. There seem to be several versions of this story, but here is the one we heard.

When Hanshin won the Japan Series for the first time in 1985, the fans went crazy. One group gathered at Nanpa Bashi over the Dōtonbori River, and as people called out the names of their favorite players, someone would jump into the river. However, when they called out the American player, Randy Bass, who helped lead the team's success, there were no foreigners in the crowd to represent him. The closest thing to a foreigner they could find was the Colonel Sanders statue in front of the nearby KFC restaurant, which they threw into the water.

The restaurant never replaced the statue, and soon afterwards Hanshin went into a deep slump. Some people claimed this was due to a jinx wrought by the Colonel himself. When, in 1992, it looked like Hanshin would win the Central League pennant, the shop finally replaced the statue. However, knowing the character of Hanshin fans, the management chained the statue to the front of the restaurant. Unfortunately, the team blew the last few critical games and failed to win the pennant. Maybe they shouldn't have kept the Colonel chained down.

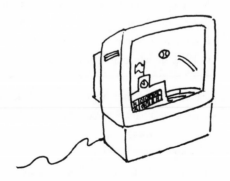

▪ 7 ▪

Fifteen More Kinki Words

By now you have certainly noticed how often the grammar and vocabulary
described thus far are used in everyday speech. Hopefully, you have tried
out some of the expressions yourself and have found people's responses
warmer and more open, or less stiff and formal. If you haven't been using
the first thirty words, why not? Don't be shy or you'll miss all the fun in
conversing. Try it out in your Japanese class. Your teacher will
undoubtedly try to correct you. Ask her how she speaks with her friends
outside of class and watch her get flustered. Yes, language study, too, is
an integral part of the Tokyo conspiracy.

Seriously, we recommend you become comfortable with the first thirty
words, since they constitute the backbone of Kansai-*ben* and are useful
in almost every situation. From this point, we concentrate more on specific
words and speech patterns that, although important to understand and
use, are somewhat more limited in application.

VOCABULARY

31. *donkusai* 鈍臭い

32. *hagaii* はがいい

33. *hokasu* ほかす

34. *kanawan* かなわん

87

VOCABULARY

35. *kannin* 堪忍
36. *makeru* 負ける
37. *shānai* しゃあない
38. *tanomu* 頼む
39. *yōke, gyōsan, yōsan* ようけ、
    仰山、ようさん
40. *zukkoi* ずっこい

GRAMMATICAL EXPRESSIONS

41. *kaina* かいな
42. *-n* ーん
43. *-ra* ーら（等）
44. *-taru* ーたる
45. *-ten* ーてん

31. *donkusai* 鈍臭い dim-witted, stupid

Donkusai translates literally as "the smell of stupidity." It means a person, or action of a person, that is dim-witted or stupid, but is usually used more in jest between friends than as an actual insult. Similar words in standard Japanese are *noroma* のろま, *nibui* 鈍い, and *guzu* 愚図.

SHIGERU: *Ah! Densha ni kasa wasurete mota.*

TADASHI: *Donkusai yatcha nā.*

茂： あっ！電車に傘忘れてもた。

正： 鈍臭いやっちゃなあ。

SHIGERU: I left my umbrella on the train.

TADASHI: You don't have your head screwed on straight.

Tadashi is teasing his friend for forgetting his umbrella. *Toroi* とろい is another Kansai word meaning a person who reacts slowly, moves slowly, or thinks slowly. *Donkusai* would be used between friends when teasing each other, while *toroi* can be used as an insult, in some contexts.

As with many adjectives, the final *-i* can be dropped and the last sound lengthened. *Donkusai* then becomes *donkusa—*. Similarly, *atsui* 暑い is often changed to *atsu—* あつ〜 and *shindoi* しんどい to *shindo—* しんど〜.

32. *hagaii* はがいい frustrating

Hagaii is a contraction of *hagayui* 歯がゆい, which literally means "itchy tooth." You know you could get rid of the itch by pulling the tooth, but you also know it would only make matters worse, so you do nothing but feel frustrated. A situation or person is *hagaii* when you know you have the means to solve a problem but can't use it. The most common usage is in reference to a person who, because of ineptitude or other reasons, is unable to do something you know you could do easily if allowed.

KENSUKE: *Oi, kotchi ni aruite kuru non, omae no akogare chau no?*
Koe kakete miiya!

KYŌTA: *E?! A, un, seyakedo, ano, sono . . .*

KENSUKE: *Aa, itte mota yan. Nani shiten nen?*
Hagaii yatcha nā, honma.

健助： おい、こっちに歩いてくるのん、お前の憧れちゃうの？
声掛けてみいや！

京太： え？！あ、うん、せやけど、あの、その...

健助： ああ、行ってもたやん。何してんねん？
はがいいやっちゃなあ、ほんま。

KENSUKE: Hey, isn't that the girl you like walking towards us?
You ought to say something to her!

KYŌTA: Huh? Well, umm . . .

KENSUKE: She's gone already. What are you doing?!
You're really frustrating!

As you can see in this example, Kensuke is getting frustrated with Kyōta because he's too shy to take Kensuke's advice and talk to the girl of his dreams. Kensuke feels he would have done a much better job if that had been the girl he liked.

An *akogare* 憧れ is someone you have a crush on. *Mii* みい attached to the *-te* form of a verb means "you should try." (See 58) *Itte mota* is equivalent to *itte shimatta* 行ってしまった in standard Japanese. (See 14) *Shiten nen* is the -ing form of *suru*. (See 45)

It is also possible to be frustrated with yourself. For example, if you are the best baseball player on the team and your team is losing, but you can't do anything about it because you are injured, you might say the following:

Jibun jishin ga hagaii.
自分自身がはがいい。
I'm frustrated with myself.

33. *hokasu*　ほかす　to throw away

Hokasu means the same as *suteru* 捨てる. Unlike many Kansai-*ben* words that are contractions or variations on the pronunciation of standard Japanese words, *hokasu* is unique to Kansai. People living outside of Kansai who are unfamiliar with this word might assume it is a contraction of *hokan suru* 保管する, meaning "to save," the opposite of *hokasu*. This can sometimes lead to misunderstandings between the Kansai office and branch offices of a company.

Kono gomi, hokasu de.
このごみ、ほかすで。
I'm throwing away this garbage.

MOTHER:	*Mō, kono zasshi iran kara, hokaso ka?*
DAUGHTER:	*Hokashi, hokashi.*
母：	もう、この雑誌要らんから、ほかそか？
娘：	ほかし、ほかし。
MOTHER:	We don't need these magazines anymore, so why don't we throw them away?

DAUGHTER: Go ahead and get rid of them.

Kono shorui, hokashitoite na.
この書類、ほかしといてな。
Throw these documents away for me, will you?

   In this example, the verb is in the *-te oku* ーておく form, *hokashite oite* ほかしておいて. As in standard Japanese, this indicates that something is set aside or prepared ahead. This form is often used to request a simple favor of someone younger or of lower standing, and is sometimes shortened to *-toite* ーといて. *Hokashitoite* is often shortened even further to *hottoite* ほっといて. Don't confuse this with *hōtte oite* ほうっておいて which is also contracted to *hottoite* and means "leave me alone." *Hokasu* is also sometimes pronounced *horu* ほる.

Mō kore, horo ka?
もうこれ、ほろか?
Should we throw these away already?

34. *kanawan*   かなわん   stuck, troubled, can't win, can't
                          stand something
This often heard word has two unrelated meanings that are both commonly used. The first meaning is "trouble" or "troublemaker," somewhat similar to *komatta* 困った. But *kanawan* can also mean "I can't win against something or someone" or "I can't stand something." The intended meaning has to be determined from the context. Here is an example of similar sentences with very different meanings.

(a) *Kanawan yatcha nā.*
かなわんやっちゃなあ。
He's a troublemaker.

In this context, *kanawan* is often shortened to *kanan*, as in *kanan yatcha nā.*

(b) *Aitsu ni wa, kanawan.*
あいつには、かなわん。
There's no way I can beat him.

Both of the above examples can be simplified to just *kanawan nā* かなわんなあ.

Related to definition (b) of *kanawan* is the feeling of not being able to stand something. In this case, *kanawan* is used in the same way as *tamaranai* たまらない, which in Kansai is pronounced *tamaran* たまらん.

Atsukute kanawan.
暑くてかなわん。
I can't stand the heat.

Atsukute tamaran.
暑くてたまらん。
I can't stand the heat.

The *kanawan* of sentence (b) is used throughout Japan, but the word is pronounced *kanawanai* かなわない outside of Kansai. The *kanawan* of sentence (a) is used exclusively in Kansai.

35. *kannin suru*   堪忍する   excuse me, forgive me,
                                        have patience
Kannin suru means the same as *kanben suru* 勘弁する, "pardon me" or

"excuse me," when asking forgiveness for a small mistake, and is often used in the context of "please have patience with me." It is sometimes shortened to *kanisuru* かにする when used in the forms *kanishite* かにして, "forgive me," and *kanishitaru* かにしたる, "I forgive you."

A young woman meeting her boyfriend who has arrived late:

NOZOMI: *Nani shitottan?! Ichi jikan mo matteten de!*

MATSUSHITA: *Kannin! Kaigi ga nobite shimoten.*

望：   何しとったん?! 1時間も待っててんで！

松下：   堪忍！ 会議が延びてしもてん。

NOZOMI: Where have you been?! I've been waiting for an hour!

MATSUSHITA: Give me a break! My meeting went late.

We recommend that Nozomi find a more considerate boyfriend.

36. *makeru*   負ける   to discount (a price)

Makeru literally means "to lose," but can also mean, especially in Kansai (although not exclusively), a special discount, usually attained by bargaining. *Benkyō suru* 勉強する is also used synonymously in this context. Neither word is used to refer to a store's standard bargain sales.

TAKAKO: *Ē nekkuresu ya nē. Nanbo yattan?*

YASUKO: *Niman en yatten kedo, ichiman rokusen en ni makete kureten.*

高子：   ええネックレスやねええ。なんぼやったん？

泰子：   二万円やってんけど、一万六千円にまけてくれてん。

TAKAKO: Nice necklace! How much was it?

YASUKO: It was originally 20,000 yen but they gave it to me for 16,000 yen.

At a flea market:

MARI:	*Kore, sen en? Mō sukoshi makete kurehen?*
SAKAI:	*Seya nā. Hona, kyūhyaku en ni maketoku wa.*
真理：	これ、千円？もう少しまけてくれへん?
堺：	せやなあ。ほな、九百円にまけとくわ。
MARI:	Is this 1,000 yen? Can you drop the price a bit?
SAKAI:	Hmm. I'll give it to you for 900 yen.

Seya nā せやなあ is equivalent to *sō da ne* そうだね. *Maketoku* まけとく is a contraction of *makete oku* まけておく where the *-te oku* form means "I'll do it for you."

This type of bargaining, although not extremely prevalent, is much more common in Kansai than elsewhere in Japan. There also seem to be more flea markets and other less formal shops, where bargaining is customary. However, most bargaining, especially at small markets, is done by asking for a reduction based on volume purchases. For example, if the list price of a piece of fish is 1,000 yen, you may be able to get two for somewhat less than 2,000 yen, or for 2,000 yen you may be able to get the shopkeeper to throw in another small piece for free. In Osaka's Nipponbashi 日本橋 (be careful with the pronunciation—Tokyo has a district written with the same characters and pronounced Nihonbashi), electronic goods can be bought at a discount for those able to bargain effectively. For example, it may be possible to convince the salesman to throw in free accessories, such as software or disks, with a computer purchase.

Bargaining is often pointed out as an indicator of the significant difference in personalities of Kansai and Kantō residents. Typical Tokyoites take pride in their ability to pay for expensive goods. Although bargain hunting may be growing in popularity all over Japan, Tokyoites would not announce to friends that they bought anything other than the best goods at full price. On the other hand, typical Kansai residents, especially those in Osaka, take pride in their ability to drive a hard bargain and to find the same goods at lower prices. It is often said this is due to the fact that Osaka has traditionally been a city of merchants, while Tokyo has been a collection of people from the countryside trying to impress each other.

So don't be embarrassed at an outdoor market, especially if you are buying more than one item. Go ahead and say *makete kurehen?* and see what happens. You might save some money and, if nothing else, have an interesting time talking with the shopkeepers in Kansai-*ben*.

37. *shānai* しゃあない   can't be helped

Shānai is a contraction of *shikata ga nai* 仕方がない or, as a language textbook might list it, *shikata ga arimasen* 仕方がありません. Literally, it means "there is no method." It is used frequently to mean "it's hopeless" or "I give up." In Tokyo it is usually contracted to *shō ga nai* しょうがない, while in Kansai it usually becomes *shānai*, with the middle *a* sound

drawn out. The word is almost always followed by *nā* なあ. Japan is sometimes referred to as the "*shō ga nai* culture" because of how quickly people give up when told they can't do something. While this refers primarily to Tokyo, *shānai* is still heard frequently in Kansai.

SUZUKI:	*Kuruma, ugokahen.*
HONDA:	*Shānai nā. Densha de iko ka.*
鈴木：	車、動かへん。
本田：	しゃあないなあ。電車で行こか。
SUZUKI:	My car's not running.
HONDA:	We've got no choice. We'll have to take the train.

In this case, *shānai* doesn't mean there is no way to go but that there is no choice in the matter. Obviously, Suzuki would rather have gone by car. Note that *ikō* 行こう is shortened to *iko* 行こ.

A telephone conversation from Umeda Station at 1 A.M.:

KENSUKE:	*Saishū densha, nogashite moten.*
	Ima kara sotchi tomari ni itte mo, ē?
KYŌTA:	*Mō shānai yatcha nā. Ē de. Kotchi, koi ya.*
健助：	最終電車、逃してもてん。
	今からそっち泊りに行っても、ええ？
京太：	もう、しゃあないやっちゃなあ。ええで。こっち、こいや。
KENSUKE:	The last train already left.
	Do you mind if I come over and stay at your place?
KYŌTA:	You screwed up again, huh? Well, come on over.

Shānai yatcha nā is equivalent to *shikata ga nai yatsu da na* 仕方がない奴だな, which means someone who ends up in hopeless situations or who screws up often. Here Kyōta is giving Kensuke a hard time.

38. *tanomu*　頼む　please; I'm counting on you

Tanomu replaces *onegaishimasu* お願いします in Kansai, especially when asking a favor of someone the same age or younger in a casual situation. It is almost always followed by the neutral sentence-ending *wa*. Older men in Osaka often pronounce it as *tanonmassa* たのんまっさ.

KAKARICHŌ:	*Kono hōkokusho, itsu made ni dekiru?*
HIKARI:	*N . . . tabun, ashita no hiru niwa . . .*
KAKARICHŌ:	*Sore de ē wa. Tanomu wa.*
係長：	この報告書、いつまでにできる？
光：	ん ... 多分、明日の昼には ...
係長：	それでええわ。頼むわ。
BOSS:	When can you have this report finished?
HIKARI:	Probably by noon tomorrow.
BOSS:	That's fine. I'm counting on you.

HONDA:	*Kankū made noshitaro ka?*
SUZUKI:	*A, honma ni? Honnara tanomu wa.*
本田：	関空まで乗したろか？
鈴木：	あ、ほんまに? ほんなら頼むわ。

HONDA: Do you want a ride to the airport?

SUZUKI: Really? Well, if you're offering, please.

Kankū is short for *Kansai Kokusai Kūkō* 関西国際空港, the international airport in Osaka Bay.

39. *yōke, gyōsan, yōsan* ようけ、仰山、ようさん a lot, many
All three of these words, identical in meaning to *takusan* 沢山, are completely interchangeable and used with roughly the same frequency. Different people, of course, tend to use one word more than the others, and there may be some regional differences in word usage.

Gyōsan kōta.
仰山買うた。
I bought a lot.

Kōta 買うた is the past tense of *kau* 買う in Kansai-*ben*.

IBARAGI: *Ashita, kaigi de happyō sena akan nen.*
Konya wa yōke sena akan koto aru wa.

HIRAKATA: *Ma, bochi-bochi ganbari!*

茨木： 明日、会議で発表せなあかんねん。
今夜はようけせなあかん事あるわ。

枚方： ま、ぼちぼち頑張り！

IBARAGI: I have to make a presentation at a meeting tomorrow.
I've got a lot to do tonight.

HIRAKATA: Well, hang in there!

YASUKO: *Hanshin hyakkaten de konna ni yōsan kaimon shiten.*

TAKAKO: *Ā, sō ka! Hanshin yūshō shitan yakke.*

泰子： 阪神百貨店で、こんなにようさんかいもんしてん。

高子： あ〜、そうか！ 阪神優勝したんやっけ。

YASUKO: Look how much I bought at Hanshin Department Store.

TAKAKO: Oh, that's right! Hanshin just won, didn't they.

If the Hanshin Tigers win the Central League pennant or the Nihon Series, Hanshin Department Store holds a special sale to celebrate the occasion. At that time, not only Tiger paraphernalia but all types of goods are on sale.

Kaimono 買物 is often shortened to *kaimon* かいもん and *tsukemono* 漬物 is shortened to *tsukemon* つけもん in casual speech.

40. *zukkoi* ずっこい cunning, sneaky

Zukkoi means the same as *zurui* ずるい or *warugashikoi* 悪賢い . This refers to a person, situation, or method that is sneaky or unfair. The final vowel is often lengthened to make it sound like zukko— ずっこ〜.

NOZOMI: *Mitsui-san, umai koto buchō ni toriitte, shōshin shitan yate.*

HIKARI: *Sō nan?! Zukkoi nā.*

望： 三井さん、うまいこと部長に取り入って、昇進したんやて。

光： そうなん？！ ずっこいなあ。

NOZOMI: I heard Mr. Mitsui got himself in good with the boss and got a promotion.

HIKARI: No way! He's pretty sneaky.

Yate means "so I heard." (See 60) *Toriiru* 取り入る means to curry favor or "brown-nose." Mitsui seems to have succeeded at gaining a promotion by currying favor with the boss.

Umai koto is equivalent to *umaku* うまく, meaning "done well." In Kansai-*ben*, some adverbs are created from the *-i* form of adjectives by adding *koto* こと. Commonly used examples are *umai koto* 上手い こと, *hayai koto* 早いこと, and *nagai koto* 長いこと, which in standard Japanese would be expressed as *umaku* 上手く, *hayaku* 早く, and *nagaku* 長く.

Nagai koto matasete gomen nā.
長いこと待たせてご免なあ。
Sorry I kept you waiting so long.

41. *kaina* かいな sentence ending expressing sarcasm, serious doubt, or a demand

This is another sentence ending unique to the Kansai dialect. *Kai* is equivalent to *ka* か, indicating a question. *Na* な, often lengthened to *nā,* なあ, is basically the same sentence ending as the *na* of word entry 28. These are frequently combined to become *kaina*. It has a rough sound and is therefore used primarily among friends or family.

(a) expressing sarcasm
Kaina is used most often to express sarcasm. However, this form is

sometimes used to express anger. It is frequently heard after *honma* ほん
ま, but can follow a verb in dictionary form.

Konna yōsan no shigoto dekiru kaina.
こんなようさんの仕事出来るかいな。
How can I possibly do all this work?

Dare ga anna kaisha iku kaina.
誰があんな会社行くかいな。
Who would want to work for such a company?

KAZUO:	*Kinō no shiken, ore manten totta de.*
HIROSHI:	*Honma kainā?*
KAZUO:	*Honma yade. Hora, mite mi!*
一雄：	きのうの試験、おれ俺満点取ったで。
宏：	ほんまかいなあ?
一雄：	ほんまやで。ほら、見てみ！
KAZUO:	I got 100% on yesterday's exam.
HIROSHI:	Yeah, right!
KAZUO:	Really. Look!

SHIGERU:	*Shachō ga, jikyū agete kureru rashii de.*
TADASHI:	*Honma kainā? Shachō gottsui kechi ya no ni.*
茂：	社長が、時給上げてくれるらしいで。
正：	ほんまかいなあ? 社長ごっついケチやのに。
SHIGERU:	I hear the boss is going to raise our hourly wages.
TADASHI:	Yeah, right! That stingy person?

In these last two examples, *honma kainā* is used as a very sarcastic
way to question the person's statement.

(b) expressing very strong doubt

In this case, *kaina* also follows the dictionary form of a verb with *-n* attached.

Anna tayorinai ko ni mise makashite daijōbu kaina?
あんな頼りない子に店任して大丈夫かいな？
Are you sure it's safe to leave the store in that kid's hands?

Dekirun kaina?
出来るんかいな？
Are you really able to do it?

Kaisha ikun kaina?
会社行くんかいな？
Are you really going into the office?

(c) expressing a demand

Kaina, when used to express a strong demand, follows a verb in the negative *-nai* －ない form with the *-ai* －あい removed.

Hayo taben kaina!
はよ食べんかいな！
Eat faster!

Sassato yaran kaina!
さっさとやらんかいな！
Do it now!

Shikkari sen kaina!
しっかりせんかいな！
Get a hold of yourself!

42. -n 　 —ん 　 (negative verb conjugation)

The negative verb conjugation *-hen* —へん or *-nai* —ない is often contracted to just *-n* —ん. This very clipped form of speech is used equally by men and women but usually only in very informal situations, such as between friends. The usual rules of negative verb conjugation apply, but *-n* is added after the *-a* base. Some verbs, such as *shiru* 知る, primarily use this negative informal ending, as in *shiran* 知らん. Other verbs, such as *aru* 有る, use only the *-hen* ending, as in *arahen* あらへん, while the majority of verbs, like *wakaru* 分かる, can use either ending, as in *wakaran* 分からん or *wakarahen* 分からへん. There is no rule for making this choice, so you will have to pick up the correct usage from listening to conversations. If you use the wrong conjugation, you are just as likely to hear *sō wa iwahen de* そうは 言わへんで as you would *sō wa iwan de* そうは言わんで.

shiran	知らん	I don't know
wakaran	分からん	I don't know
iran	要らん	I don't need it, no thanks

iwan	言わん	don't say
tsukawan	使わん	don't use
kanawan	かなわん	can't beat
dekin	できん	can't do

A rising intonation at the end turns this form into a question.

MIYAZAWA:	*Shiran?*
TAKESHITA:	*Shiran.*
宮沢：	知らん？
竹下：	知らん。
MIYAZAWA:	Do you know?
TAKESHITA:	I don't know.

43. *-ra* ーら （ー等） (plural form)

-Ra added to a noun indicates the plural, as in groups of people. Although this is common in written Japanese, it is used much more frequently in spoken Kansai dialect, while *-tachi* ー達 is more common in standard Japanese speech.

atashira	あたしら	us (women)
uchira	うちら	us
orera	俺ら	us (men)
anokora	あの子ら	those kids
otchanra	おっちゃんら	the old men

None of these examples would be used in standard Japanese, although other words using *-ra*, such as *bokura* 僕ら, are not uncommon. The word *uchi* うち is often used in Kansai to indicate "me." Therefore, *uchira* うちら means "us" and *uchira no* うちらの means "our."

44. -taru ーたる   I'll do it for him/her/you

The verb conjugation -taru is a contraction of -te yaru ーてやる, meaning "I will do it for you" or "I will do it for him/her." This conjugation is formed by attaching -ru to the -ta form of the verb.

Fuku kōtaru.
服買うたる。
I'll buy those clothes for you.

Ashita mukae ni kitaru wa.
明日迎えに来たるわ。
I'll come pick you up tomorrow.

Meshi tsukuttaru.
飯作ったる。
I'll make you something to eat.

Aitsu, dotsuitaru!
あいつ、どついたる！
I'm going to punch that guy out!

Yūtaru.
ゆうたる。
I'll go tell them for you.

One frequently used variation of this form is -taro ーたろ, a contraction of -shite yarō ーしてやろう, which has a slightly softer sound but essentially the same meaning as -taru. The only difference in these two expressions is that -taro can be used in both interogatory and declarative sentences.

Kane, kashitaro ka.
金、貸したろか？
Do you want me to lend you some money?

Jitensha naoshitaro.
自転車直したろ。
I'll fix the bicycle for you.

Aitsu, nakashitaro ka?
あいつ、泣かしたろか？
I'll teach him a lesson!

    Kansai people often use the phrase above, which literally means "I'm going to make him scream," when they get angry with someone.

    Because *-taru* sounds somewhat rude, many women prefer to use *-tageru* －たげる, a contraction of *-shite ageru* －してあげる, which is more polite than *-shite yaru*.

I'll lend you some money.
Kane, kashitaru wa.	金、貸したるわ。	(male)
Okane, kashitageru wa.	お金、貸したげるわ。	(female)

Gohan tsukuttageru wa.
ご飯作ったげるわ。
I'll make you something to eat.

Okane, kashitage.
お金、貸したげ。
Please loan him some money.

Another verb conjugation is created by contracting *-te yari* ーてやり to *-tari* ーたり and *-te yare* ーてやれ to *-tare* ーたれ. Both forms have the same meaning of "please do this for him" or "you should do this," but *-tare* sounds rougher than *-tari* and is used primarily by men.

Let him borrow that.
Kashitare.   貸したれ。   (male)
Kashitari.   貸したり。   (female)

Kanojo ni denwa shitari.
彼女に電話したり。
You should call her.

45. *-ten*   ーてん   (past tense verb conjugation)
This verb conjugation, created by adding *-n* to the *-te* form of the verb, forms the past tense equivalent to *-ta n da* ーたんだ in standard Japanese. It is used when the speaker wants to add some emphasis or feeling to the sentence. The plain *-ta* ーた past tense form is used to state a fact.

Kinō, gakkō itten.
きのう、学校行ってん。
I went to school yesterday.

Kekkon shiten.
結婚してん。
I got married.

Ano fuku, imōto ni ageten.
あの服、妹にあげてん。

I gave those clothes to my younger sister.

While *-ten* by itself is a past tense verb conjugation, it becomes the progressive (-ing) form when combined with *nen*, as in *-ten nen* ーてんねん. This form is equivalent to *-te iru* ーている in standard Japanese.

These past tense and -ing forms are easily confused by non-natives. Note the difference in the following examples:

Nani shiten?
何してん？
What did you do?

Nani shiten nen?
何してんねん？
What are you doing?

Here are some more examples of the *-ten nen* form:

Manga yonden nen.
漫画読んでんねん。
I'm reading the comics.

Repōto kaiten nen.
レポート書いてんねん。
I'm writing a report.

Ima, Matsushita-kun to tsukiatten nen.
今、松下君と付き合ってんねん。
I'm currently dating Matsushita.

Makudo de baito shiten nen.
マクドでバイトしてんねん。
I'm working part time at McDonald's.

    Baito is short for *arubaito* アルバイト , a part-time job.

■ 8 ■
Example Conversations III

Conversation 1: At the office, the boss asks the office ladies to do all the drudgery.

1 KAKARICHŌ: *Warui kedo, kono tana no shorui zenbu hokashitotte kurehen ka?*
2 HIKARI, NOZOMI: *Ha—i.*
3 KAKARICHŌ: *Tanomu wa. (heya o deru)*
4 HIKARI: *Mō! Ano hito, kanawan nā.*
5 NOZOMI: *Honma, honma. Konna yōsan no shorui atashira dake de hakoberu kai na.*
6 HIKARI: *Kō yū zatsuyō bakkari atashira ni oshitsukete,*
7   *jibun wa oishii shigoto bakkari yatten nen kara.*
8   *Aitsu, zukkoi wa.*
9 NOZOMI: *Honma. Hara tatsu wa.*

1 係長：   悪いけど、この棚の書類全部ほかしとってくれへんか？
2 光、望： は〜い。
3 係長：   頼むわ。（部屋を出る）

4 光：　　　　もう！あの人、かなわんなあ。
5 望：　　　　ほんま、ほんま。こんなようさんの書類あたしらだけで
　　　　　　　運べるかいな。
6 光：　　　　こうゆう雑用ばっかりあたしらに押し付けて、
7 　　　　　　自分はおいしい仕事ばっかりやってんねんから。
8 　　　　　　あいつ、ずっこいわ。
9 望：　　　　ほんま。腹立つわ。

1 BOSS:　　　　I know it's a pain, but would you mind getting rid of all
　　　　　　　the documents in this book shelf?
2 HIKARI, NOZOMI: O—kay.
3 BOSS:　　　　Thanks. I'm counting on you. (He leaves the room.)
4 HIKARI:　　　I can't believe it! I can't stand that guy!
5 NOZOMI:　　　Really! Does he really believe we can carry all
　　　　　　　those documents?
6 HIKARI:　　　He always pushes the drudgery off on us and
7 　　　　　　keeps all the interesting work for himself.
8 　　　　　　That guy's a sneaky dog.
9 NOZOMI:　　　Yeah, he gets me so angry.

Line 1: As elsewhere in Japan, requests often start off with *warui kedo,* which means "it's bad of me to ask, but . . ." or "I know it's a pain, but . . ." even when the person doesn't really believe he is asking for much. In this case, as the bookcase is filled with company reports, *hokasu* probably means not simply throwing them away but shredding all the documents as well.

Line 2: The women's response, *ha—i,* with the drawn out sound, indicates they aren't really happy about carrying out the request but, realizing they have no choice in the matter, agree reluctantly.

Line 3: *Tanomu* roughly means "thanks" in this situation. In standard Japanese, the boss would have said *onegai* お願い.

Line 4: Once the boss is gone, the women are free to vent their anger to each other.

Line 5: *Atashi* あたし is a feminine contraction of *watashi* 私. The *-ra* attached to the end changes the meaning from "me" to "us." *Kaina* is used to express sarcasm toward the boss, who believes the two women will be able to move all the documents by themselves.

Line 6: *Zatsuyō* 雑用 is routine work, in this case, all the boring drudgery. *Oshitsukeru* 押し付ける is a standard Japanese word that means to force something onto another person.

Line 7: *Oishii* usually refers to good-tasting food, but is also used to describe work that is favorable or profitable to oneself.

Conversation 2: Between two sweethearts.

Nozomi has been waiting a long time for Matsushita, her boyfriend, to meet her at Nanba Station. He finally arrives and runs toward her.

1 MATSUSHITA: *Gomen nā. Nagai koto matashite shimote.*

2 NOZOMI: *Mō! Shiran!*

3 MATSUSHITA: *Machiawase no jikan, kanchigai shiteten.*

Gomen hā!

4 NOZOMI: *Donkusa—.*
5 MATSUSHITA: *Ohiru ogottaru kara kannin shite.*
6 NOZOMI: *Shānai na. Seyattara, yurushitaru wa.*

1 松下 ：   ご免なあ。長い事待たしてしもて。
2 望 ：   もう！知らん！
3 松下 ：   待ち合わせの時間、勘違いしててん。
4 望 ：   どんくさ〜。
5 松下 ：   お昼おごったるから堪忍して。
6 望 ：   しゃあないな。せやったら、許したるわ。

1 MATSUSHITA: I'm sorry. I made you wait for a long time.
2 NOZOMI: I'd given up already.
3 MATSUSHITA: I made a mistake in our meeting time.
4 NOZOMI: That was pretty stupid.
5 MATSUSHITA: I'll buy lunch. Please forgive me.
6 NOZOMI: I guess there's no choice. In that case, I'll forgive you.

Line 2: *Mō! Shiran!* means here that he's not worth the trouble of knowing anymore.

Line 3: *Shitotten* しとってん is the past tense of *shitoru* しとる, the progressive (-ing) form of *suru* する. This is equivalent to the standard Japanese *shite ita* していた. Similarly, *tabetotten* 食べとってん means "I was eating" and *mitotten* 見とってん means "I was watching."

Line 5: *Ohiru* お昼, which only means "afternoon," is used here as short for *ohiru gohan* お昼ご飯 or lunch. *Ogoru* おごる means "to treat someone to something" and is used much more often than *gochisō* 御馳走 to indicate buying a meal for someone. *Ogoru* is also used when treating someone to a movie or even taxi fare. *Gochisōsama deshita* 御馳走様でした, usually said after a meal to the person who prepared it or paid for it, is sometimes replaced with *gottsuosan* ごっつおさん by men in Kansai. This is often shortened to *gossosan* ごっそさん, or even further to *gossan* ごっさん.

Line 6: *Seyattara* is equivalent to *sō dattara* meaning "in that case." *Se* or *so* replaces the standard *sō* そう and *yattara* replaces *dattara*. *Yurushitaru* 許したる is the shortened form of *yurushite ageru* 許してあげる.

Conversation 3: A housewife returns from the market carrying two bags of rice. She is greeted by her neighbor, Takako.

1	TAKAKO:	*Okusan, sonna yōsan okome kōte kite, donai shihattan?*
2	YASUKO:	*Yā, okusan, asoko no mise de, hitofukuro sen en no okome,*
3		*"futafukuro kau kara" yūtara*
4		*kyūhyaku en zutsu ni makete kuretan yo.*
5	TAKAKO:	*Atashi, sakki sen en de kōte shimota wa.*
6		*Okusan ni wa kanawan wa. Kondo, atashi mo yatte miru wa.*

1	高子：	奥さん、そんなようさんお米こうてきて、どないしはっ
		たん？
2	泰子：	やあ、奥さん、あそこの店で、一袋千円のお米、
3		「二袋買うから」言うたら
4		九百円ずつに負けてくれたんよ。
5	高子：	あたし、さっき千円でこうてしもたわ。
6		奥さんにはかなわんわ。今度、あたしもやってみるわ。

1	TAKAKO:	You sure bought a lot of rice. What's up?
2	YASUKO:	Oh, hi. I was at this shop where they had rice for 1,000 yen per bag,
3		so I said, "how about if I buy two bags,"
4		and she gave them to me for 900 yen per bag.
5	TAKAKO:	I just paid 1,000 yen.
6		I can't beat you. Next time I'll try that myself.

Line 1: Housewives often address each other as *okusan*, meaning "wife." *Donai suru* どないする is hard to translate but roughly means "what will you do?" In this case, the past tense of the respectful *-haru* form is attached along with a final *-n*, short for *no*, which turns this into a question. Thus, *donai shihattan* どないしはったん means something like "what did you do?" or "what's up?" These women are talking politely to each other. In less formal conversations, *donai shitan* どないしたん is commonly heard.

Line 2: *Yā* is used to say hello or to express mild surprise at meeting someone.

Line 4: The housewife bargained for a discount by buying two bags of rice at a cheaper rate than for a single bag. Unlike Tokyoites, she is proud of her ability to find a bargain.

Line 6: *Kanawan* means "I am unable to win against you." Takako is showing her respect for Yasuko's intelligence and good sense in getting a reduced price for the rice, although she may say this sarcastically.

Conversation 4: Yasuko with her crying child, Mako, and her neighbor, Takako.

1	MAKO:	*Bie—n!*
2	TAKAKO:	*Okusan, donai shitan?*
3	YASUKO:	*Yā, kono ko, taisetsu na tegami hokashite shimotan yo.*
4		*Honma ni donkusai ko ya nen kara. Dare ni nitan yaro.*
5	TAKAKO:	*Tanomu kara, kani shitatte.*
6		*Mako-chan mo muri ni nakushitan chau nen kara.*
7		*Nā, kawaisō ni konna ni yōsan namida, nagashite.*
8	YASUKO:	*Shānai nā.*

1	麻子：	ビエ〜ン！
2	高子：	奥さん、どないしたん？
3	泰子：	やあ、この子、大切な手紙ほかしてしもたんよ。
4		ほんまに鈍臭い子やねんから。誰に似たんやろ。

5	高子：	頼むから、かにしたって。
6		まこちゃんも無理に無くしたんちゃうねんから。
7		なあ、可哀想にこんなにようさん涙、流して。
8	泰子：	しゃあないなあ。

1	MAKO:	Waaaa!
2	TAKAKO:	What's wrong, Yasuko?
3	YASUKO:	This child threw away an important letter of mine.
4		She's really stupid. I wonder who she takes after?
5	TAKAKO:	Please forgive her.
6		She lost it by accident, didn't she?
7		She's already cried so much and looks so sad.
8	YASUKO:	Oh well, I guess it's spilled milk now.

Line 2: As in the previous example, *donai shitan* means "what's happened?" or "what's wrong?"

Line 4: *Dare ni nitan yaro* 誰に似たんやろ literally translates as "who does she resemble?" The mother is implying that the child certainly doesn't take after her.

Line 5: Here *tanomu* means "I'm asking you to . . ." *Kani* is short for *kannin*, meaning "have patience." *Shitatte* したって is a contraction for *shite agete* してあげて, meaning "please do something for someone." Put together, this sentence means "please be patient with her" or "please forgive her."

Line 8: In this situation, *shānai* indicates that Yasuko has no choice but to forgive her child, but she is doing it only as a favor to Takako.

■ 9 ■

Kinki Cuisine

The Kansai area is well known for certain foods. Osaka is famous for *okonomiyaki*, Kyoto is known for *yudōfu* and *nishin soba* (noodles with herring), Kobe for Kobe beef, Nada for sake, and Akashi for *Akashi-yaki*. Even foods found throughout Japan are prepared differently here and have names different from the ones used in Tokyo. So while you are here, make sure you try Kansai cuisine and remember to use the correct local names.

Okonomi お好み

Okonomiyaki お好み焼き, usually referred to as just *okonomi*, is considered the "kinkiest" of Kansai Cuisine. Japanese like to call it "Japanese pizza," but this is misleading since, beyond its round shape and varied toppings, it has little to do with pizza. Its texture is much closer to that of pancakes. *Okonomiyaki* restaurants are numerous throughout Kansai, relatively inexpensive, and have a casual atmosphere that makes them an ideal place to dine with friends. Some restaurants cook the food on a hot plate in the middle of your table or at the counter. Like pizza, toppings such as squid, shrimp, pork, beef, and cheese can be

118

ordered to taste. The most popular and traditional toppings are pork and squid, referred to as *butatama* 豚玉 and *ikatama* いか玉, respectively. Many restaurants serve a variation called *modan-yaki* モダン焼き, which is *okonomiyaki* with *yakisoba* noodles. *Okonomi* is also easy and fun to make at home, and is especially suitable for small parties. Here is how to make it:

Ingredients: Cabbage, egg, flour, *okonomiyaki* sauce, *tororoimo* (とろろ芋 yams), *katsuobushi* (鰹節 dried bonito flakes), *aonori* (青海苔 green nori flakes), *tenkasu* (fried dough), and toppings such as shrimp, squid, bacon, cheese, potato, corn, mochi, beef, etc.

Preparation: Cut the cabbage into small strips. Mix the cabbage, egg, flour, grated *tororoimo*, *tenkasu*, and water. Heat the hot plate and spread a small amount of oil in the pan. Pour the mixture into a circle, like a pancake and about two centimeters high. Wait about 3 minutes and add toppings. When the bottom turns light brown, flip over. When that side is brown, flip over again and apply sauce, *katsuobushi*, *aonori*, and mayonnaise, if you like. Turn down the heat on the hot plate. Cut into small pieces and eat.

Takoyaki タコ焼き **and** *Akashi-yaki* 明石焼き

Tako means "octopus" and *takoyaki* is a popular ping-pong ball-shaped

snack made from eggs, flour, and soup stock, with a chunk of octopus in the middle and coated with sauce and *aonori*. To make it at home, a special *takoyaki* pan is required. It is much easier to buy it from the little carts that dot the streets near train and subway stations, especially at night. *Akashi-yaki* is similar, but it is more egg-flavored, and is dipped into a thin soup before eating. If you're still hungry after eating *Akashi-yaki*, you can drink the soup. The name comes from the city of Akashi, which is on the sea coast just west of Kobe and famous for its octopus.

Udon うどん

Udon is popular throughout Japan, but the *udon* in Kansai tastes slightly different than that found elsewhere. The broth color is much lighter, almost clear. Japanese visitors to Kansai are often surprised that they can see the noodles inside the soup and mistakenly add soy sauce to darken the soup. In Kansai, *udon* is more popular than *soba*.

Kobe Beef 神戸ビーフ

The beef from cows in the Kobe area is well known throughout the world as being especially tender and tasty. These cows are supposedly fed beer and massaged every day in order to improve the tenderness of the beef. Although cheaper than in Tokyo, even in Kobe the beef is quite expensive, and essentially reserved for people on expense accounts. However, Kobe beef or other *wagyū* (和牛 Japanese beef) for *shabu-shabu* しゃぶしゃぶ can be had for only slightly outrageous prices at the local supermarket. *Shabu-shabu* is also enjoyable for parties, and is extremely easy to make.

Ingredients: Thinly sliced beef, *hakusai* (白菜 Chinese cabbage), *tōfu*, *shiitake*, *enoki*, bean thread, chrysanthemum leaves, and *ponzu* and sesame sauce.

Preparation: Boil water in a *nabe* pot. Add *hakusai*, *shiitake*, and *tōfu*. Dip beef one slice at a time in the boiling water for a few seconds until it turns brownish-red. Dip in sauce and eat.

Other Local Specialties

Tetchiri: The *fugu* (河豚 globefish) version of *shabu-shabu*.

Ikanago: Small fish boiled hard in sugar and soy sauce. Famous in Hyogo Prefecture.

shabu-shabu

Tonkatsu: Fried pork cutlet found throughout Japan, but especially good in Kansai.

Ethnic foods, especially Korean and Chinese, are well known here because of the large population of ethnic Koreans and Chinese. Kobe has a Chinatown in the Motomachi district known as Nankin Machi, while Osaka has a Koreatown in Tsuruhashi, which is famous for its *yaki-niku,* or Korean barbeque.

Local Names for Other Foods

A few other varieties of food that are found throughout Japan go by different names in Kansai.

LOCAL NAME	STANDARD NAME
buta-man 豚マン	*niku-man* 肉マン
kantō-daki 関東煮	*oden* おでん
nankin 南京	*kabocha* かぼちゃ
kashiwa かしわ	*tori-niku* 鳥肉
bara-zushi バラ寿司	*chirashi-zushi* 散らし寿司
otsukuri お造り	*sashimi* 刺し身
kitsune キツネ	*kitsune-udon* キツネうどん
mamushi まむし	*unagi-don* うなぎどん
tanuki タヌキ	*kitsune-soba* キツネそば
reikō 冷コー	*aisu-kōhii* アイスコーヒー (ice coffee)
hotto ホット	*hotto-kōhii* ホットコーヒー (hot coffee)
miikō ミーコー	*miruku-kōhii* ミルクコーヒー (café au lait)
retii レティー	*remon-tii* レモンティー (lemon tea)
makudo マクド	*makudonarudo* マクドナルド (McDonald's)

■ 10 ■
Final Fifteen Words To Master Kinki Speech

While this is our last set of fifteen words and grammatical expressions, it by no means exhausts the range of speech in Kansai. We hope it provides a good introduction to the language and makes it possible to understand most of the language spoken in the Kinki region of Japan.

VOCABULARY

46. *erai* えらい
47. *ichibiri* いちびり
48. *ikezu* いけず
49. *irau* いらう
50. *nangi* 難儀
51. *sara* 新 (さら)
52. *shōmonai* しょうもない
53. *toko* とこ
54. *yaru* やる
55. *yossha* よっしゃ

GRAMMATICAL EXPRESSIONS

56. *do-* どー
57. *kate* かて
58. *-mii* ーみい
59. *non* のん
60. *yate* やて

46. *erai* えらい   very, tiring, magnificent

Erai has many different usages, making it difficult to grasp its exact meaning in the context of a conversation. Its most basic meaning is as an intensifier, similar to the standard Japanese *sugoi* 凄い, *totemo* とても, *hijō ni* 非常に, or *taihen* 大変. As such, it often has negative connotations. By itself, it usually means "tired" or "tiring," and is a synonym for *shindoi* しんどい. However, it is also used in standard Japanese as a synonym for *rippa* 立派, meaning a superior person, or something great.

Erai kotcha! Ashita shiken ya no ni benkyō shitehen wa!
えらいこっちゃ！ 明日試験やのに勉強してへんわ！
Oh no! I've got a test tomorrow and I haven't studied at all!

HIRAKATA:	*Ashi donai shitan?*
IBARAGI:	*Sukii de kega shitan ya.*
HIRAKATA:	*Sora, erai kotcha nā.*
枚方：	足どないしたん？
茨木：	スキーで怪我したんや。
枚方：	そら、えらいこっちゃなあ。

HIRAKATA:	What happened to you?
IBARAGI:	I injured my leg skiing.
HIRAKATA:	That's horrible.

Erai kotcha is probably the most typical usage. *Kotcha* is short for *koto ya* ことや, equivalent to the standard *koto da* ことだ, meaning "thing" or "event." Together, the expression means "horrible" or "that's too bad." The closest equivalent in standard Japanese is *taihen da* 大変だ. *Sora* そら is a contraction of *sore wa* それは.

Erai ame ya nā.
えらい雨やなあ。
It's really pouring.

Erai tenki ya nā. Ōyuki ya wa.
えらい天気やなあ。大雪やわ。
This is really awful weather. It's snowing hard.

In these two examples above, the meaning of *erai* is closer to the standard Japanese *hidoi* ひどい, and includes an awareness of the largeness or greatness of nature.

Erai asa hayo kara, kaigi sun nen nā.
えらい朝はよから、会議すんねんなあ。
I've got a meeting very early in the morning.

In this example, *erai* is the same as *totemo* とても or *hijō ni* 非常に meaning "very," but includes the connotation that this early meeting is unusual and unwelcome.

Kyō, mutcha erakatta wa.
今日、むっちゃえらかったわ。
Today was really rough.

Here, *erai* is synonymous with *shindoi*. (See 21) For an even stronger expression, the two words can be combined, as in *erai shindokatta* えらいしんどかった.

47. *ichibiri* いちびり dolt, clown, easily excitable person
Ichibiri is a derogatory term used to describe someone who is too easily elated, implying stupidity. The best English translation might be "clown," "spaz," or "dolt." The closest expression in standard Japanese is *ochōshimono* お調子者.

Anna ichibiri aite ni sunna.
あんないちびり相手にすんな。
Just ignore that clown.

Sunna すんな is a shortened form of *suru na* するな, meaning "don't do that."
The verb form of *ichibiri* is, not surprisingly, *ichibiru* いちびる, which means to clown around or act stupid.

Ichibiru na!
いちびるな！
Quit clowning around!

This can be shortened to *ichibinna!* いちびんな！

48. *ikezu* いけず mean, nasty

Ikezu is an adjective used to describe a mean or nasty person, or it is used as a noun to describe something nasty someone has done. It is never said aloud to the person being described except as a joke.

Aitsu, honma ni ikezu ya na.
あいつ、ほんまにいけずやな。
That guy's really mean.

Sonna ikezu, iwantoite.
そんないけず、言わんといて。
Don't say such mean things.

49. *irau* いらう touch, meddle with
This word means to touch, either physically or in an abstract sense, as in to "mess with" something. The closest equivalent words in standard Japanese are *ijiru* いじる and *sawaru* 触る.

Kore, irote mo ē?
これ、いろてもええ？
Do you mind if I touch this?

Sore irotara akan de.
それ、いろたらあかんで。
Don't mess with that.

In this example, it is difficult to tell if the physical or abstract meaning of *irau* is intended. The speaker could be telling the other person not to put their hands on something. But he could also be telling the person not to ruin the item. The past tense of *irau* いらう is *irota* いろた, and *irattara* いらったら is simplified to *irotara* いろたら.

Kitanai te de irawantoite.
汚い手でいらわんといて。
Don't touch that with your dirty hands.

A sister is telling her brother not to touch the item until he cleans his hands. Here *-toite* －といて means "please" or "do it" and is used in a casual way. It is often used among friends or siblings, and can be further contracted to *-totte* －とって.

50. *nangi* 難儀 difficult, annoying
Nangi is the Kansai version of *muzukashii* 難しい or *mendōkusai* 面倒臭い and is usually followed by *ya nā* やなあ. It is accompanied by plenty of air sucking through the teeth, and can be considered a somewhat polite way to say "no" or "you're really imposing on me." It is used mostly by men and older people.

HIRASHAIN: *Ashita no kaigi, shusseki shiharimasu ka?*
KACHŌ: *Sora, nangi ya nā. Ashita, mō tsumatten nen.*
平社員： 明日の会議、出席しはりますか？
課長： そら、難儀やなあ。明日，もうつまってんねん。
EMPLOYEE: Are you going to attend tomorrow's meeting?
BOSS: That's a problem. My schedule tomorrow is already full.

In this situation, the boss is really saying "no."

Nangi na yatcha.
難儀なやっちゃ。
He's really picky.

Here, *nangi* can mean "difficult," as in "he is a difficult person."

Erai nangi na koto ni natte shimota.
えらい難儀な事になってしもた。
This situation has become extremely difficult.

51. *sara* 新 (さら) new
People throughout Kansai tend to say *sara* instead of *atarashii* for "new."
This is especially prevalent when talking about goods.

Kono kaban, sara ya nen.
この鞄、さらやねん。
This is a new briefcase.

The most common usage of *sara* is probably when it is combined
with *hin* 品 to make *sarappin* さらっぴん (新品), which means "new
goods." It is also sometimes pronounced *sarapin* さらぴん.

Kono kaban, sarapin ya nen.
この鞄、さらぴんやねん。
This is a new briefcase.

For added emphasis, *ma* 真 is often added to *sara* to create *massara*
まっさら. This can be translated as "brand-new."

Kono kaban, massara ya nen.
この鞄、まっさらやねん。
This briefcase is brand-new.

52. *shōmonai* しょうもない uninteresting, boring, trifling
Shōmonai has two related meanings, the most common of which is "uninteresting" or "boring," similar to *omoshirokunai* 面白くない or *tsumaranai*

つまらない in standard Japanese. The other meaning, "unimportant" or "trifling," is equivalent to *kudaranai* 下らない or *taishita koto nai* 大した事ない in standard Japanese. It is sometimes pronounced *shomonai* しょもない, *shomona—* しょもな〜, or *shōmunai* しょうむない.

Shōmonai bangumi ya nā.
しょうもない番組やなあ。
That show's boring.

Shōmonai gyagu.
しょうもないギャグ。
A stupid joke.

In the above two examples, *shōmonai* means something boring or uninteresting. In the following examples, it describes something that is trifling, even though it may not be boring or uninteresting. Note that *hayo* is the Kansai pronunciation for *hayaku* 早く.

Anna shōmonai kaisha, hayo yamete shimai!
あんなしょうもない会社、はよ辞めてしまい！
Quit that useless company as soon as you can!

Sonna shōmonai koto de nayamu koto arehen wa.
そんなしょうもない事で悩むことあれへんわ。
There's no need to worry about such a trifling matter.

53. *toko* とこ place
Toko is a contraction of *tokoro* 所. While this literally means "place," it is used frequently in expressions indicating possession. While this

contraction is used throughout Japan, the high frequency with which Kansai residents use it, even when it seems to add no extra meaning to the sentence, makes this a part of Kansai-*ben*. Kansai people also shorten the *no* の that grammatically should precede *toko* to *n* ん, or drop it completely.

anta toko	あんたとこ	your house/your family/your office
uchi toko / uchintoko	うちとこ／うちんとこ	my house/my family/my office
uchintoko no niwa	うちんとこの庭	our garden

Kōbe, honma ni ē toko ya.
神戸、ほんまにええとこや。
Kobe is a really nice place.

Minami, yōke asobu toko aru de.
ミナミ、ようけ遊ぶとこあるで。
There're plenty of places to have fun in Nanba.

Anna hito ga yōsan oru toko, yō sumarehen wa.
あんな人がようさんおるとこ、よう住まれへんわ。
I can't live somewhere where there are that many people.

54. *yaru* やる give

While *yaru*, meaning "to give" (don't confuse this with the homonym that means "to do"), is actually part of standard Japanese, it has a broader usage. In standard Japanese, this word is only used in reference to giving something to a plant or animal, or maybe a child. For example, *inu ni esa o yaru* 犬に餌をやる means "feed the dog." However, in Kansai this word can be used instead of *ageru* あげる when giving something to a person of equal or lower status. However, it does sound rude and is used almost exclusively by men, while most women stick with the more polite *ageru*. It is frequently followed by the ending *wa*.

Ore, mō kono wāpuro tsukawan kara yaru wa.
俺、もうこのワープロ使わんからやるわ。
I'm not using this word processor anymore, so I'll give it to you.

Kono hon, mō iran kara yaru wa.
この本、もう要らんからやるわ。
I'm finished with this book so you can have it.

MIKA:	*Hoshikattara yaro ka?*
TOMOKO:	*Ē wa. Iran.*
美香：	欲しかったら、やろか？
友子：	ええわ。要らん。
MIKA:	Do you want this?
TOMOKO:	That's okay. I don't need it.

55. yossha よっしゃ yes, okay, great!
Yossha is a very common way of expressing anything from simple assent to extreme pleasure.

HIRAKATA:	*Omae ni kono shigoto makasu wa.*
IBARAGI:	*Yossha, makashitoki.*
枚方：	お前にこの仕事任すわ。
茨木：	よっしゃ、任しとき。
HIRAKATA:	I'm entrusting you with this job.
IBARAGI:	Okay. Leave it to me.

ANNOUNCER: *Hanshin, manrui hōmuran!*

TORAKICHI: *Yossha! Yattā!*

アナウンサー：阪神、満塁ホームラン！

トラキチ：　　よっしゃ！やったあ！

ANNOUNCER: Hanshin just hit a grand slam home run!

TORAKICHI: Yes! They did it!

Yattā is a very common expression of pleasure at success. It is a form of *yatta* やった, the past tense of *yaru* やる, meaning "did." A literal translation might be "They did it!" or "I did it!"

56. *do-* ど－ (prefix for emphasis)

This is a prefix used before nouns and adjectives to intensify their meaning. It is usually used with words that are derisive or show scorn, and make this effect even stronger.

do-aho	どアホ	a true idiot
do-inaka	ど田舎	pure countryside
do-sukebe	どすけべ	a real pervert

Ano ko no keshō, itsumo do-gitsui nā.
あの子の化粧、いつもどぎついなあ。
That girl always wears too much make-up.

In some cases, *do-* merely intensifies the meaning without adding any negative connotations.

do-mannaka　　　　　　ど真ん中　　　　　　the exact center

57. *kate*　かて　(same as *-temo, demo, mo,* or *de sae*)
Kate is a grammatical particle that is difficult to translate into English, but the usual meaning is similar to "even if . . ." It is used in place of the standard Japanese particles *demo* でも, *mo* も, *de sae* でさえ, and the verb conjugation *-temo* ーても.

Sonna koto yūta kate, dekihen mon wa dekihen nen.
そんな事言うたかて、出来へんもんは出来へんねん。
No matter what you say, what's impossible is impossible.

Ima kara yatta kate, muri chau?
今からやったかて、無理ちゃう？
Even if you start now, it's already hopeless, isn't it?

In the above two examples, *kate* is used in the same manner as *-temo* ーても in standard Japanese. This particle is placed after the *-tta* ーった form of the verb. In the following two examples, *kate* is used after a noun, and has the same meaning as *mo* も, *de sae* でさえ, or *demo* でも. *Sonnan* そんなん is equivalent to *sonna koto* そんなこと.

Sonnan shōgakusei kate shitteru wa.
そんなん小学生かて知ってるわ。
Even elementary school kids know that.

Atashi kate iya ya wa, sonnan.
あたしかていやや わ、 そんなん。
I don't want to do that, either.

58. -mii －みい try it

Mii is an auxilliary verb conjugated to the *-te* form of another verb and means "ought to try it." Depending on the tone, it can also be a casual way of saying "do it." It is derived from *miru* 見る and is essentially the same as the standard Japanese *-shite mite* －してみて.

Hosokawa-han, kono ika kutte mii. Umai de.
細川はん、このイカ食ってみい。旨いで。
You ought to try this squid. It's really good!

Kono bangumi, mite mii. Omoroi de.
この番組、見てみい。おもろいで。
You ought to see this program. It's really interesting!

Jōshi ni sōdan shite mii.
上司に相談してみい。
What if you tried talking this over with your boss?

In these three examples, the speaker is recommending that the person do something, and the sentence ends with a flat or rising tone. However, *mii* can also be used to express a demand, especially in the rhetorical sense.

Omae, iitai koto arun nara, yūte mii!
お前、言いたいことあるんなら、ゆうてみい。
Hey buddy, if you've got something to say to me, say it!

As you might expect by this point, *-mii* can be shortened even further by leaving off the final *-i*.

Kono hon, mite mi.
この本、見てみ。
Take a look at this book.

Similarly, other standard Japanese verbs in the *-te* form, when asking for something, are often expressed in the *-i* form in Kansai.

kii 来い	come	*kotchi kii* こっち来い		come here
kii 着い	wear	*kore kii* これ着い		try this on
shii しい	do	*denwa shii* 電話しい		you should call
yomii 読みい	read	*kyōkasho yomii* 教科書読みい		read your textbook

59. *non* のん (a) possessive conjunction, (b) particle indicating recurring event, (c) sentence ending for questions

(a) *Non* is used to indicate the possessive form of a noun when the item isn't specified. This is equivalent to *no* の or *no mono* のもの in standard Japanese.

uchi non うちのん mine

| *aitsu non* | あいつのん | that guy's |
| *Nagata non* | 長田のん | Nagata's |

Uchi non tsubureten nen.
うちのん潰れてんねん。
Mine's broken.

HIKARI:	*Kore, dare non?*
NOZOMI:	*Jibun non chau?*
光：	これ、誰のん？
望み：	自分のんちゃう？
HIKARI:	Whose is this?
NOZOMI:	It's yours, isn't it?

In Kansai, *jibun* 自分 often means "you" instead of "I."

(b) Another usage of *non* is as a particle that indicates a recurring event, and is equivalent to *mono* もの or *koto* こと.

Gakkō iku non, tarui nā. Yametoko ka nā.
学校行くのん、たるいなあ。やめとこかなあ。
I've got to go to school. What a hassle. Maybe I won't go.

Note that *tarui* たるい means the same as *mendōkusai* 面倒臭い , "a pain in the neck" or "a hassle." *-Toko* ーとこ is a contraction of *-te okō* ーておこう.

Sonna hito to dēto suru non, iya ya wa.
そんな人とデートするのん、いややわ。
There's no way I would date that guy!

(c) *Non* is also used as a sentence ending to indicate a question. In this case, it is equivalent to *no* in standard Japanese.

Kaisha ikehen non?
会社行けへんのん？
You're not going to work?

Mō tabehen non?
もう食べへんのん？
You're not eating?

Konnan sanman en mo sun non?
こんなん三万円もすんのん？
They charge 30,000 yen for this?

60. *yate* やて so I heard
Yate is equivalent to the standard Japanese *datte* だって, which has many usages, but essentially means "it was said . . ." or "I heard that . . . ," indicating hearsay information. Hopefully, a few examples will clarify its usage.

Ashita, ame yate.
明日、雨やて。
It's supposed to rain tomorrow.

Fukyō no tame ni kyūryō katto yate.
不況の為に給料カットやて。
I heard our salaries are going to be cut due to the recession.

Nozomi-chan, kekkon shitan yate.

望ちゃん、結婚したんやて。

I heard that Nozomi got married.

Shitan yate is often contracted further to *shitente*. Therefore the news about Nozomi's marriage can be said, as follows:

Nozomi-chan, kekkon shitente.

望ちゃん、結婚してんて。

We were planning to finish on that final good news about Nozomi, but then realized there is one more important word to save for last.

61. *honja* ほんじゃ see you later

Honja is used in the same manner as *hona*, *honnara*, and *sonnara*, explained in word entry 18. But *honja* is also the most common way to say farewell to friends in Kansai. Its meaning is much closer to "see you later" than "goodbye." Women often say *hona* ほな instead, but use *honja*, as well. The standard *sayōnara* さようなら is usually pronounced *sainara* さいなら in Kansai, but as elsewhere, it can have the meaning of "goodbye forever." So instead, we would rather leave you with this:

PALTER:	*Honja, mata na.*
HORIUCHI:	*Hona, mata ne.*
ポーター：	ほんじゃ、またな。
堀内：	ほな、またね。
PALTER:	Until next time, see you later.
HORIUCHI:	See you.

▪ 11 ▪

Example Conversations IV

Conversation 1: Two office ladies having a conversation over dinner at a *robatayaki*.

1	NOZOMI:	*Saikin donai?*
2	HIKARI:	*Sore ga nā, atarashiku uchitoko no ka ni kita hito, ikezu de nā.*
3		*Hito no shōmonai misu, mitsukete wa erai sawagitatete na.*
4	NOZOMI:	*Nangi na hito ya nā.*
5	HIKARI:	*Kinō kate, hito no shorui irōte,*
6		*gucha-gucha ni shite kureten.*
7		*Mattaku erai me ni ōta wa.*
8	NOZOMI:	*Onaji ka no senpai ni yūte mitara, dō ya non?*
9	HIKARI:	*Un. Yūte miten kedo,*
10		*tada "mō choi gaman shite mii" yate.*

1	望：	最近、どない？
2	光：	それがなあ、新しくうちとこの課に来た人、いけずでなあ。

140

3		人のしょうもないミス、見つけてはえらい
		騒ぎ立ててな。
4	望：	難儀な人やなあ。
5	光：	昨日かて、人の書類いろうて、
6		ぐちゃぐちゃにしてくれてん。
7		全くえらい目におうたわ。
8	望：	同じ課の先輩にゆうてみたら、どうやのん？
9	光：	うん。ゆうて見てんけど、
10		ただ「もうちょい我慢してみい」やて。

1	NOZOMI:	How have you been?
2	HIKARI:	Well, we've got this new guy in my department and he's really mean.
3		He makes a big fuss out of even the smallest mistakes people make.
4	NOZOMI:	This guy's a real pain, huh?
5	HIKARI:	Yesterday, he messed with the papers on my desk
6		and got them all mixed up.
7		I had a really bad day.
8	NOZOMI:	Have you tried talking to your *senpai* in the department?
9	HIKARI:	Yeah, I tried saying something but
10		all she answered was "try to be patient for a bit longer."

Line 2: *Uchitoko no ka* うちとこの課, means "my department." *Toko* doesn't really have any meaning here except to help the flow of the sentence.

Line 3: *Sawagitateru* 騒ぎ立てる means "to make a fuss." *Erai* えらい is used as an intensifier here.

Line 7: *Hidoi me ni au* ひどいめに会う is an expression that means "had a bad day." In Kansai, this expression is changed to *erai me ni au* えらいめに会う. The past tense of *au* in Kansai is *ōta* おうた.

Line 10: *Choi* ちょい is equivalent to *chotto* ちょっと. *Yate* やて at the end indicates that the previous sentence is a quote. *Mii* みい means "try to," as in "try to be patient."

Conversation 2: Tomoko and Mika at Mika's apartment.

1	TOMOKO:	*Konna ni yōsan no fuku, donai shitan?*
2	MIKA:	*Tōkyō ni hikkoshi shita tomodachi ni mōten kedo,*
3		*uchitoko semai yaro.*
4		*Oku toko, komatten nen.*
5	TOMOKO:	*Uwā. Sara no fuku made aru yan.*
6	MIKA:	*Hoshikattara yaro ka.*
7		*Demo saizu au ka dō ka ippen kite mii.*
8	TOMOKO:	*Anta wa kiihin non?*
9	MIKA:	*Kite min kate, awahen non wakatten nen.*
10		*Sono ko, mechakucha hosoi ko ya nen.*

1	友子：	こんなにようさんの服、どないしたん？
2	美香：	東京に引っ越しした友達にもうてんけど、
3		うちとこ狭いやろ。
4		置くとこ、困ってんねん。
5	友子：	うわあ。さらの服まであるやん。
6	美香：	欲しかったらやろか。
7		でもサイズ合うかどうか、一遍着てみい。
8	友子：	あんたは着いひんのん？
9	美香：	着てみんかて、合わへんのん分かってんねん。
10		その子、めちゃくちゃ細い子やねん。

1	TOMOKO:	What's with all these clothes?
2	MIKA:	I got them from a friend who just moved to Tokyo, but
3		my room is pretty small.

4		I don't know where to put them all.
5	TOMOKO:	Wow. There are even some new clothes in here.
6	MIKA:	If you want any of them, I'll give them to you.
7		Why don't you try one on and see if it fits you?
8	TOMOKO:	You're not going to wear them?
9	MIKA:	Even without trying them on I know that they won't fit.
10		She's really thin.

Line 2: *Mōten* もうてん is the past tense of *morau* もらう, which means "to receive."

Line 3: In this case, *uchitoko* うちとこ means "my home."

Line 4: *Okutoko* 置くとこ is short for *oku tokoro* 置く所, which means "a place to put things."

Line 6: *Yaro ka* やろか is a very informal way to say "I'll give you." In more polite speech, she would have said *ageru wa* あげるわ.

Line 7: *Kite mii* 着てみい means "try it on."

Line 8: *Non* のん at the end of this sentence indicates that this is a question.

Line 9: The *non* in the middle of the sentence works like "that" in English. Here, it adds the meaning "that" to "I know 'that' they won't fit." *Kite min* 着てみん is the Kansai version of *kite minai* 着てみない, which means "not try them on." *Kate* かて in this case means "even if" or "even though." Together they mean "even without trying them on." The equivalent phrase in standard Japanese would be *kite minakute mo* 着てみなくても.

Conversation 3: A mother and daughter discussing *omiai* お見合い, a formally arranged date.

1	MOTHER:	*Anta, nande anna ē hito kotowattan?*

2   *Tochi motteru shi, ē kaisha ni tsutometeru shi,*
3   *se kate takōte, kakko yokatta yanai?*
4 DAUGHTER: *Tochi motteru yūta kate, anna do-inaka yan.*
5   *Sore ni ano hito metcha ibatten nen.*
6   *"Boku mawari kara eriitotte iwareterun desu" yate.*
7   *Aho chau ka? Shōmonai otoko ya wa, zettai.*
8 MOTHER: *Sonnan yūta kate anta, jibun no toshi kangaete mii.*
9   *Ikutsu ya omoten non?*
10   *Otōsan kate, "Anta o yome ni yaru made shinarehen"*
           yūten nen yo.
11 DAUGHTER: *Hona, otōsan zettai shinarehen wa.*
12 MOTHER: *Nangi na musume ya nā.*

1 母：   あんた、なんであんなええ人断ったん？
2   土地持ってるし、ええ会社に勤めてるし、
3   背かてたこうて、かっこよかったやない？
4 娘：   土地持ってるゆうたかて、あんなど田舎やん。
5   それにあの人めっちゃ威張ってんねん。
6   「僕、周りからエリートって言われてるんです」やて。
7   あほちゃうか？　しょうもない男やわ、絶対。
8 母：   そんなんゆうたかて、あんた、自分の年考えてみい。
9   いくつや思てんのん？
10   お父さんかて、「あんたを嫁にやるまで死なれへん」ゆ
           うてんねんよ。
11 娘：   ほな、お父さん絶対死なれへんわ。
12 母：   難儀な娘やなあ。

1 MOTHER: Why did you turn down such a great guy?
2   He owns his own land, has a good job,
3   he's even tall and good looking, isn't he?

4 DAUGHTER:	Maybe he owns land, but it's way off in the countryside.
5	And he's real stuck-up.
6	"The people around me say I'm elite," he says.
7	Pretty stupid, huh? He's a complete nothing.
8 MOTHER:	Think about your age before you talk like that.
9	How old do you think you are?
10	Your father said, "I can't die until you're married."
11 DAUGHTER:	Well, in that case, there's no chance that he'll ever die.
12 MOTHER:	What a pain in the neck daughter I have.

Line 3: Here k*ate* かて has the same meaning as *datte* だって or *mo* も, namely that he is **even** tall. *Takōte* たこうて is the Kansai pronunciation for *takakute* 高くて, meaning "high" or, as in this case, "tall." *Kakko* かっこ is equivalent to *kakkō* 格好, meaning "appearance." *Yanai* やない is equivalent to *janai* じゃない.

Line 4: The *do-* どー added to *inaka* 田舎 can mean either that the land her suitor owns is way out in the boonies or that she is showing her scorn for any place other than the city.

Line 8: *Jibun* 自分 is used by the mother to mean "you." *Mii* みい is used as a softer way to demand something, somewhat similar to *nasai* なさい in standard Japanese.

Conversation 4: Two authors at the end of the day. We hope to hear from you again, so we'll leave you with this last example.

1 PALTER:	*Kono hon kaku non, dō yatta?*
2 HORIUCHI:	*Nnn, shindokatta kedo, iro-iro tanoshikatta wa.*
3 PALTER:	*Hori-chan yō ganbatta nā.*
4 HORIUCHI:	*Pōtā-han kate. Demo mō owari ya nen nā.*

5   *Kore kara, donai suru?*

6 PALTER: *Seya nā. Do ya!? Tsugi no hon demo kako ka?*

7 HORIUCHI: *Ē nā, sore.*

8 PALTER: *Yossha, ashita kara mata ganbaro!*

9 HORIUCHI: *Un. Hona, ashita ne.*

10 PALTER: *Honja.*

1 ポーター： この本書くのん、どうやった？

2 堀内： ん〜。しんどかったけど、色々楽しかったわ。

3 ポーター： 堀ちゃんよう頑張ったなあ。

4 堀内： ポーターはんかて。でももう終わりやねんなあ。

5 これから、どないする？

6 ポーター： せやなあ。どや！？　次の本でも書こか？

7 堀内： ええなあ、それ。

8 ポーター： よっしゃ、明日からまた頑張ろ！

9 堀内： うん。ほな、明日ね。

10 ポーター： ほんじゃ。

1 PALTER: What did you think of writing this book?

2 HORIUCHI: Well, it was a lot of work, but I enjoyed it, too.

3 PALTER: You really worked hard.

4 HORIUCHI: So did you. But now we're done.

5   What will we do after this?

6 PALTER: Hmm. I've got it! How about writing another book?

7 HORIUCHI: That's a good idea.

8 PALTER: Okay! We'll start right in on it tomorrow!

9 HORIUCHI: Well then, I'll see you tomorrow.

10 PALTER: See you then.

■ Dictionary ■

Note: Sample sentences appear when the entry word is not dealt with extensively in the main text. Standard Japanese equivalents appear in parentheses with each entry.

ahokusa アホくさ stupid thing (*bakarashii* 馬鹿らしい)
Ahokusa! Ashita, asa shichiji kara kaigi yate.
アホくさ！明日、朝7時から会議やて。
That's so stupid! Holding a meeting at 7 in the morning tomorrow!

ahō, aho 阿呆、アホ (See 1) fool, stupid, foolish (*baka* 馬鹿)

akan あかん (See 2) no, no good, bad, useless, impossible, expletive
(dame 駄目)

akko あっこ over there (*asoko* あそこ)
Uchi toko, akko ya nen.
うちとこ、あっこやねん。
My place is over there.

anta, ansan, antahan あんた、あんさん、あんたはん you; contraction
of *anata* あなた (*kimi* 君)

Anta ni wa kankei nai wa.

あんたには関係ないわ。

That's none of your business.

arahen あらへん doesn't exist, not here (*nai* 無い)

Gohan mō arahen wa.

ご飯もうあらへんわ。

There is no more rice left.

benkyō suru 勉強する to discount a price (*makeru* 負ける)

bochi-bochi ぼちぼち (See 16) so-so, not bad, not good

chau ちゃう (See 3) no, wrong, different (*chigau* 違う); sentence ending
meaning "isn't that right?" (*ja nai?* じゃない？)

choi, chō, cho ちょい、ちょお、ちょ (*chotto* ちょっと)

Choi matte.

ちょい待って。

Hold on a second.

dabo ダボ asshole (fighting word); contraction of *do-aho* どアホ

de で (See 26) exclamatory sentence ending (*yo* よ , *zo* ぞ)

dekka でっか contraction of *desu ka* ですか

denna でんな contraction of *desu na* ですな (*desu ne* ですね)

Kyō, honma ni atsui denna.

今日、ほんまに暑いでんな。

It is really hot out today.

do- どー (See 56) prefix to add emphasis to nouns and adjectives

donai どない how is it? (*dō* どう)

Kono kutsu, donai?

この靴、どない？

How do I look in these shoes?

donai shitan どないしたん what's wrong? what happened? (*dōshita no* どうしたの)

Kinō donai shitan?

昨日、どないしたん？

What happened to you yesterday?

donai sho どないしょ what should I/we do? (*dō shiyō* どうしよう)

Shimekiri made mikka shika arehen. Donai sho?

締め切りまで３日しかあれへん。どないしょ。

I've only got three days until the deadline. What am I going to do?

donai suru どないする what are you/we going to do? (*dō suru* どうする)

Kare no koto, donai surun?

彼のこと、どないするん？

What are you going to do about your boyfriend?

donai yatta どないやった how was it?

Eiga donai yatta?

映画、どないやった？

How was the movie?

donkusai 鈍臭い (See 31) dim-witted, stupid (*nibui* 鈍い)

doshitan どしたん contraction of *dōshita no* (*dōshita* どうした)

Konna sugoi kuruma, doshitan?

こんなすごい車、どしたん？

How did you get such a nice car?

dotsuku どつく to punch, to hit (*naguru* 殴る)

Aitsu, dotsuitaro ka!

あいつ、どついたろか！

I want to punch that guy out!

dō shō mo nai どうしょうもない hopeless, impossible, give up (*shō ga nai* しょうがない)

Ame yakara, dō shō mo nai.

雨やから、どうしょうもない。

It's raining, so there's nothing we can do.

doya どや what do you think? how is that? contraction of *dōya* どうや

Omoikkiri makete, 3,800 en de doya?

思いっきり負けて、三千八百円でどや？

How about if I give you my best offer of 3,800 yen?

ē ええ (See 4) good, that's enough (*ii* いい, *yoi* 良い)

ēkakkoshii ええ格好しい person who puts on airs, pretentious

egui えぐい disgusting, nauseating

Kono aisu kuriimu no iro, egui nā.

このアイスクリームの色、えぐいなあ。

The color of this ice cream is nauseating.

erai えらい (See 46) very (*hijō ni* 非常に, *totemo* とても); tiring (*taihen* 大変; *shindoi* しんどい); magnificent (*rippa* 立派)

gametsui がめつい greedy (*yokubari* 欲張り)

gana がな sentence ending used as intensifier

Gakko ikan to akan gana.

がっこ行かんとあかんがな。

You absolutely have to go to school.

geiko 芸子 exclusive Kyoto geisha, or geisha (in general)

geinin 芸人 professional entertainer or person with a talent for making people laugh

gera ゲラ a person who laughs hard (*warai jōgo* 笑い上戸)

Gion 祇園 traditional district near Kawaramachi in Kyoto famous for geiko

goneru ごねる to whine, to complain
Nanbo gonete mo ame agehen de.
なんぼごねても飴あげへんで。
No matter how much you complain, I'm not going to give you any candy.

gossan ごっさん → *gottsuosan*

gossosan ごっそさん → *gottsuosan*

gottsuosan, gossosan, gossan ごっつおさん、ごっそさん、ごっさん
thanks for the food (*gochisōsama deshita* 御馳走様でした)

gottsui ごっつい (See 17) very, big

gyōsan 仰山 (See 39) a lot, many (*takusan* 沢山)

hagaii はがいい (See 32) frustrating

-han －はん (See 27) Mr./Ms. (*-san* －さん)

Hanshin 阪神 Hanshin Tigers baseball team; Hanshin Railway; Hanshin Department Store; Osaka-Kobe region; Hanshin horse racing track in Takarazuka

-haru －はる (See 11) honorific verb conjugation (*nasaru* なさる)

hayo はよ early, quickly (*hayaku* 早く、速く)
Kono shigoto, hayo sena akan nen.
この仕事、はよせなあかんねん。
We have to do this job quickly.

-hen ーへん (See 12) negative verb conjugation (*-nai* ーない)

hokasu ほかす (See 33) to throw away (*suteru* 捨てる)

hona, honara ほな、ほなら (See 18) in that case, if so, then, see you later

honde ほんで then, after that, and (*sorede* それで, *sorekara* それから)
Ōsaka itte, Kyōto itte, Shiga itte, honde kaette kiten.
大阪行って、京都行って、滋賀行って、ほんで帰って来てん。
I went to Osaka, Kyoto, Shiga, then came back.

hondemo ほんでも but, nevertheless (*sore demo* それでも)
Hondemo suki ya nen.
ほんでも好きやねん。
But I like it.

honja ほんじゃ (See 61) see you later, goodbye, in that case (*soreja* それじゃ)

honma ほんま (See 5) really (*hontō* 本当)

honnara ほんなら in that case, if so, then (*sore nara* それなら)

horu ほる (See 33) throw away (*suteru* 捨てる)
Ano pitchā gottsu hayai tama horu de.
あのピッチャーごっつ速い玉ほるで。
That pitcher throws really fast.

ichamon いちゃもん complaint, whine (*monku* 文句)

Ichi-ichi, ichamon tsukentotte.
いちいち、いちゃもん付けんとって。
Stop being so contrary.

ichibiri いちびり (See 47) dolt, clown (*ochōshi mono* お調子者)

ichibiru いちびる (See 47) to clown around, to act stupid

ikezu いけず (See 48) mean, nasty (*ijiwaru* 意地悪)

ikkomo いっこも not even a little bit, not at all; preceding negative
verb or adjective (*zenzen* 全然)
Kono manga, ikkomo omoronai.
この漫画、いっこもおもろない。
This comic isn't even the least bit interesting.

iko 行こ let's go (*ikō* 行こう)
Ashita Nanba iko.
明日難波行こ。
Let's go to Nanba tomorrow.

irau いらう (See 49) to touch, to meddle with (*ijiru* いじる, *sawaru*
触る)

irachi いらち irritable person

itchan いっちゃん number 1, most (*ichiban* 一番)
itchan aho
いっちゃんアホ
stupidest

itchomae いっちょまえ self-important (*ichininmae* 一人前)
Anoko itchomae ni sebiro kiteru wa.
あの子いっちょまえに背広着てるわ。
That kid looks full of himself in that suit.

jibun 自分 you (*anata* あなた)

Jibun, kanto-daki suki?

自分、関東煮好き？

Do you like oden?

kaina かいな (See 41) sarcastic sentence ending; sentence ending
     expressing doubt; demand

kakko かっこ appearance, shape (*kakkō* 格好)

Kyō kirei na kakko shiteru yan.

今日、きれいな格好してるやん。

You look nice today.

kamahen, kamehen かまへん、かめへん don't mind (*kamawanai*
     構わない)

Karite ē ka nā?

借りてええかなあ？

Do you mind if I borrow this?

Kamahen, kamahen.

かまへん、かまへん。

I don't mind.

kanawan かなわん (See 34) troubled, stuck; can't win against someone
     or something (*kanawanai* かなわない)

kannin suru, kani suru 堪忍する、かにする (See 35) excuse me, have
     patience with me (*kanben suru* 勘弁する)

Kansai 関西 same as *Kinki*; same as *Kei-Han-Shin*

kate かて (See 57) (*mo* も, *-te mo* ーても, *demo* でも, or *de sae* でさえ)

katsu-katsu かつかつ barely surviving, barely in time (*giri-giri* ぎり
     ぎり)

Kongetsu no seikatsu, katsu-katsu ya.

今月の生活、かつかつや。

I have barely enough money to survive this month.

Kawaramachi 河原町 main shopping and entertainment district of central Kyoto

Kei-Han-Shin 京阪神 tri-city region of Kyoto, Osaka, and Kobe

kēhen, kiihen, kiihin けえへん、きいへん、きいひん don't come (*konai* 来ない)

Konban, kotchi kēhen ka?

今晩、こっちけえへんか？

Why don't you come over here tonight?

kettai けったい strange, unusual, comical (*hen* 変, *myō* 妙)

Sorya, kettai na kotcha nā.

そりゃ、けったいなこっちゃなあ。

That's really strange.

Kinki 近畿 southern half of Honshū, including Osaka-fu, Kyoto-fu, Mie-ken, Shiga-ken, Hyogo-ken, Nara-ken, and Wakayama-ken

Kita キタ Osaka region around Umeda and Osaka Stations

koeru 肥える gain weight (*futoru* 太る)

Saikin, mata koeten.

最近、また肥えてん。

I've put on weight again recently.

koeteru 肥えてる fat, overweight (*futotte iru* 太っている)

Ano koeteru hō ga, uchi no buchō ya.

あの肥えてる方が、うちの部長や。

That fat guy over there is our boss.

kokeru こける fall down, fall over, trip (*taoreru* 倒れる, *korobu* 転ぶ)
  Uchi no ko, kokete ōkega shitan yo.
  うちの子、こけて大怪我したんよ。
  My daughter fell down and hurt herself pretty badly.

kora, korya こら、こりゃ contraction of *kore wa* これは
  Kora, akan de.
  こら、あかんで。
  This is no good.

kosobai こそばい ticklish (*kusuguttai* くすぐったい)

kotcha こっちゃ thing or event; contraction of *koto ya* ことや (*koto da* ことだ)
  Nan no kotcha.
  何のこっちゃ。
  What the &%$ is that?

Kōshien 甲子園 baseball stadium where the Tigers play; national high school baseball tournament; town in Nishinomiya where Kōshien stadium is located

kōte こうて buy; verb *-te* form (*katte* 買って)
  Gyōsan kōte shimota.
  ぎょうさんこうてしもた。
  I bought more than I planned to.

kōta こうた bought (*katta* 買った)
  Kuruma, kōtan?
  車、こうたん?
  Did you buy a car?

-mahen －まへん semi-polite negative verb conjugation (*-masen* －ません)

Konban, mājan shimahen ka?
今晩、マージャンしまへんか？
Do you want to play mahjong tonight?

maido 毎度 (See 6)　hello

maiko 舞子　girl training to become a geiko

makashi, makashitoki 任し、任しとき　leave it to him; I'll take care of it
Sono shigoto, kōhai ni makashi.
その仕事、後輩に任し。
Let your trainee take care of that job.

makeru 負ける (See 36) to discount a price

-makka －まっか　contraction of *-masu ka* －ますか
Okāsan itehari makka?
お母さんいてはりまっか？
Is your mother home?

manzai 漫才　stand-up comedy

manzai-shi 漫才師　stand-up comedian

massara 真っ新　brand-new
Sono fuku, massara chau?
その服、まっさらちゃう？
Those are brand-new clothes, aren't they?

-masse －まっせ (*-masu yo* －ますよ)
Hayo ikan to, okuremasse.
早よ行かんと、遅れまっせ。
You'd better hurry or you'll be late.

mecha めちゃ (See 7) very (*sugoku* 凄く); reckless, disorganized
　　(*mecha-kucha* めちゃくちゃ)

megeru めげる to break (*kowareru* 壊れる)
　　Kono jitensha megetoru.
　　この自転車めげとる。
　　This bicycle is broken.

metcha めっちゃ (See 7) very (*sugoku* 凄く)

-mii, mi －みい、み (See 58) try it, do it (*mite* みて)

Minami ミナミ region of Osaka near Nanba Station

mokkai もっかい once more, again; contraction of *mō ikkai* もう一回
　　Mokkai jūsho oshiete.
　　もっかい住所教えて。
　　Tell me your address again.

-mon －もん contraction of *mono* もの
　　Tsukemon, kuu ka?
　　漬もん、食うか？
　　Do you want some *tsukemono* (pickled vegetables)?

-mota －もた (See 14) contraction of *-shimota* (*shimatta* しまった)

morota もろた received (*moratta* もらった)
　　Sono ame, dare kara morotan?
　　その飴、だれからもろたん？
　　Who did you get that candy from?

mōkarimakka, mōkattemakka もうかりまっか、もうかってまっか
　　(See 19) how are you? how's business?

mōta もうた received (*moratta* もらった)

mucha むちゃ (See 7) same as mutcha, mecha; reckless, disorganized (*mucha-kucha* むちゃくちゃ)

mutcha むっちゃ (See 7) very (*sugoku* 凄く)

-n ーん (See 42) negative verb conjugation (*-nai* ーない)

-n ーん sentence ending for questions; contraction of *no*
Ashita, gorufu ikun?
明日、ゴルフ行くん？
Are you going golfing tomorrow?

na, nā な、なあ (See 28) sentence ending (*ne*, ね)

nan なん sentence ending; contraction of *nano* なの
Sore nan nan?
それ何なん？
What is that?

nanbo なんぼ (See 8) how much (*ikura* 幾ら)

nangi 難儀 (See 50) difficult, no (*muzukashii* 難しい, *mendōkusai* 面倒臭い)

Naniwa なにわ old name for Osaka

nanmo 何も nothing; contraction of *nani mo* なにも followed by negative verb or adjective
Rēzōko n naka, nanmo nokottehen.
冷蔵庫ん中、なんも残ってへん。
There's nothing left in the refrigerator.

nanya 何や (*nanka* 何か)
Nanya wakaran kedo, kakarichō erai fukigen yawa.
何や分からんけど、係長えらい不機嫌やわ。

I don't know what's wrong, but the manager is in a really bad mood.

naosu なおす clean up, put away (*katazukeru* 片付ける)

Kono zasshi, hondana ni naoshitoite.

この雑誌、本棚になおしといて。

Please put away these magazines in the bookcase.

nen ねん (See 13) neutral sentence ending

neya ねや sentence ending used for question or statement (*no da* のだ , *no* の)

Nani shiten neya?

何してんねや？

What are you doing?

non のん (See 59) possessive conjunction (*no mono* のもの , *no* の);
particle indicating recurring event (*mono* もの , *koto* こと);
sentence ending for questions (*no?* の？)

nukasu ぬかす to say (vulgar form) (*iu* 言う)

Nani aho na koto nukashiton ja?

何アホな事ぬかしとんじゃ？

What kind of stupid things are you saying?

nukui 温い warm (*atatakai* 暖かい)

Kono heya, nukui na.

この部屋、温いな。

This room's warm.

obahan おばはん middle-aged lady (*obasan* おばさん)

ochokuru おちょくる tease, make fun of (*karakau* からかう)

Aitsu, itsumo hito no koto ochokunnen.

あいつ、いつも人のことおちょくんねん。

He always makes fun of me.

ōkini 大きに (See 9) thank you (*arigatō* ありがとう)

omoroi おもろい (See 20) interesting (*omoshiroi* 面白い)

oru おる (See 10) is, exists (*iru* いる)

ossan おっさん middle-aged man (*ojisan* おじさん)
  Ano ossan, yopparatteru wa.
  あのおっさん、酔っ払ってるわ。
  That guy's drunk.

otchan おっちゃん middle-aged man (*ojisan* おじさん)
  Yaoya no otchan, itsumo makete kuren nen.
  八百屋のおっちゃん、いつも負けてくれんねん。
  The guy at the fruit stand always gives me a discount.

ōta おうた (*atta* 会った、合った)
  Hikōki no naka de, yūmei jin ni ōten.
  飛行機の中で、有名人におうてん。
  I met a famous person on the plane.

pachiru, pakuru ぱちる、ぱくる to steal (*nusumu* 盗む)

-ra 一等（ら）(See 43) suffix to make pronoun plural (*-tachi* 一達)

Rokkō 六甲 Mt. Rokko

Rokkō Oroshi 六甲颪 Hanshin Tigers fight song; wind that blows down
  from Mt. Rokko

sainara さいなら goodbye (*sayōnara* さようなら)

sakaini さかいに because, for that reason (*kara* から, *no de* ので)
  Hona, mata kuru sakaini.

ほな、また来るさかいに。
Well then, I'll be back.

-san －さん (See 29) suffix used in greetings (*-sama* －さま, *gozaimasu* ございます)

Sannomiya 三宮 refers to the downtown area of Kobe; main train station in Kobe

sara 新 (さら) (See 51) new (*atarashii* 新しい)

sarappin, sarapin 新品 new goods or product
Furii māketto demo, yōke sarappin utteru de.
フリー マーケットでも、ようけ新品売ってるで。
They even sell a lot of new stuff at the flea market.

sēhen せえへん don't do (*shinai* しない)
Kinō nanmo sēhen katta.
昨日何もせぇへんかった。
I didn't do anything yesterday.

sen せん don't (*shinai* しない)
Shinpai sen kate, daijōbu ya.
心配せんかて、大丈夫や。
Don't worry, it will be fine.

sesshōna 殺生な don't kill me, have mercy on me
Kinō kashita sanman en, ashita kaeshite ya.
昨日貸した3万円、明日返してや。
Tomorrow, pay me back the 30,000 yen that I lent you yesterday.

Sonna sesshōna!
そんな殺生な！
Have mercy on me!

seya せや (*sō* そう)

   Seya seya.

   せや、せや。

   That's right.

seyakara せやから (*sō dakara* そうだから)

   Seyakara yametoki, yūta ya nai no.

   せやから止めとき、ゆうたやないの。

   That's why I said you shouldn't do that.

seyakedo せやけど (*sō dakedo* そうだけど)

seyattara せやったら　same as *soyattara*

shānai しゃあない (See 37) it can't be helped, hopeless (*shikata ga nai* 仕方がない)

shibaku しばく　punch (*naguru* 殴る); do (*suru* する)

shii しい　do it (*shinasai* しなさい)

   Hayo shukudai shii.

   はよ宿題しい。

   Do your homework now.

shiihin しいひん　don't do (*shinai* しない); same as *sēhen*

shimota しもた (See 14) (*shimatta* しまった)

shindoi しんどい (See 21) tiring, hard

shitente してんて　I heard . . . happened; contraction of *shitan yate* したんやて (*shitan datte* したんだって)

   Yoshihara-han, tenshoku shitente.

   吉原はん、転職してんて。

   I heard Mr. Yoshihara found a new job.

shitatte したって please do it for him/her (*shite agete* してあげて)

Denwa shitatte.

電話したって。

Please call him.

sho, shiyo しょ、しよ (*shō* しょう)

Sō sho.

そうしょ。

Let's do that.

shōmonai, shomonai しょうもない、しょもない (See 52) uninteresting; trifling

sonai そない so much, too much (*sonna ni* そんなに); in that manner (*sono yō ni* そのように)

Sonai mecha-kucha iwankate, ē ya nai.

そないめちゃくちゃ言わんかてええやない。

You don't need to criticize me quite that much.

Sonai shitoki.

そないしとき。

Do it that way.

sonnara そんなら (See 18) in that case, if so, then (*sore nara* それなら)

sonnan そんなん that is (*sonna no* そんなの, *sonna koto* そんな事)

Sonnan zukkoi wa.

そんなん、ずっこいわ。

That's pretty sneaky.

sora, sorya そら、そりゃ contraction of *sore wa* それは

Sora, akan wa.

そら、あかんわ。

That's no good.

sōya, soya そうや、そや (*sō da* そうだ)
　　Sora sōya.
　　そら、そうや。
　　That's right.

sōyattara, soyattara そうやったら、そやったら in that case (*sō dattara* そうだったら, *sore dattara* それだったら)
　　Sōyattara, yameru wa.
　　そうやったら、やめるわ。
　　In that case, I give up.

suki ya nā, sukkya nā, suki ya nen, sukkya nen 好きやなあ, 好っきゃなあ、好きやねん、好っきゃねん (See 22) like

sunmahen, sumahen, sunmasen, suman すんまへん、すまへん、すんません、すまん excuse me (*sumimasen* すみません)
　　Kono aida wa, honma ni sunmahen deshita.
　　この間は、ほんまにすんまへんでした。
　　I'm really sorry about what happened.

Taigāsu タイガース Hanshin Tigers

takōte たこうて tall, high, expensive (*takakute* 高くて)
　　Sutēki wa takōte, metta ni taberarehen.
　　ステーキはたこうて、めったに食べられへん。
　　Steak is expensive, so I can't eat it very often.

-tan ーたん *-n* added to standard *-ta* form of past tense (*-ta* ーた)
　　Nani shitan?
　　何したん？
　　What did you do?

tanomu 頼む (See 38) please, I'm counting on you (*onegaishimasu* お願いします)

-tari, -tare 　ーたり、ーたれ　(See 44) please do this for him/her (contraction of *-shite yari*)

-taru, -taro 　ーたる、ーたろ　(See 44) I'll do it for him/her/you (contraction of *-shite yaru*)

-tatte 　ーたって　please do it for him/her (*-te agete* ーてあげて)
Shokuji tsukuttatte.
食事作ったって。
Please make him something to eat.

-tēna, -tēnā, -tēya 　ーてえな、ーてえなあ、ーてえや　casual request; attached to *-te* form of verb (*-te* ーて)
Mise, tetsudatēna.
店、手伝ってえな。
Would you give me a hand at the shop?

-ten 　ーてん　(See 45) past tense verb conjugation (*-tan da* ーたんだ)

-ten nen 　ーてんねん　(See 45) progressive (-ing) verb conjugation (*-te iru* ーている, *-teru* ーてる)

tereko 　てれこ　mixed up, in the wrong order (*tagai chigai* 互い違い)
Shorui ga tereko ni natteru wa.
書類がてれこになってるわ。
You put the pages in the wrong order.

-toki 　ーとき　do it; contraction of *-te oki* ーておき (*-nasai* ーなさい)
Otōsan ni ayamattoki!
お父さんに謝っとき！
Apologize to your father!

toko 　とこ　(See 53) place (*tokoro* 所)

-toko −とこ contraction of *-te okō*−ておこう (*-te oku* −ておく)

Kyō, nomi ni iku no yametoko.

今日、飲みに行くのやめとこ。

Let's forget about going out drinking tonight.

-ton −とん progressive form of verb conjugated to *-te* form with *-te* changed to *-ton* (*-te iru* −ている)

Nani tabeton?

何食べとん？

What are you eating?

Tora-kichi 虎キチ devoted Hanshin Tigers fan

-toru −とる progressive verb conjugation (*-te iru* −ている, *-teru* −てる)

Nani shitorun?

何しとるん？

What are you doing?

-totte −とって contraction of *-toite* (*-te oite* −ておいて)

Bideo tottotte.

ビデオ録っとって。

Please set the VCR for me.

tsuburereru 潰れる break (*kowareru* 壊れる)

Kono shāpen tsubureteru wa.

このシャーペンつぶれてるわ。

This pencil's busted.

tsukōte, tsukote つこうて、つこて to use; *-te* form of *tsukau* 使う (*tsukatte* 使って)

Moshi yokattara, kore tsukōte.

もしよかったら、これつこうて。

Feel free to use this if you like.

uchi うち I (*watashi* 私)

Uchi no kuruma.
うちの車。
My car.

Uchi toko.
うちとこ。
My home/office/spouse.

uchira うちら we, our (*watashitachi* 私達)
Uchira no purojekuto.
うちらのプロジェクト。
Our project.

umai 旨い delicious (*oishii* 美味しい)
Kono resutoran, umai de.
このレストラン旨いで。
This restaurant is really good.

uttōshii 鬱陶しい (See 23) gloomy, dreary

wa わ (See 30) neutral sentence ending (*yo* よ)

waya わや screw-up, ruined (*mecha-kucha* めちゃくちゃ)
Konna ame no naka, kimono kitara waya ni naru wa.
こんな雨の中、着物着たらわやになるわ。
If I wear my kimono out in this rain, it will be ruined.

ya や (See 15) (*da* だ)

yakedo やけど (*dakedo* だけど)

yan やん (*jan* じゃん , *janai no* じゃないの)
Ano hito, kakko ē yan.
あの人、かっこええやん。

That guy's handsome.

-yan －やん suffix attached to names between friends (*-kun* －君)

yanai やない (*janai* じゃない)
Ano mise shimatterun yanai?
あの店、閉まってるんやない？
That shop's closed, isn't it?

yanka やんか (*janai ka* じゃないか)
Anta unten dekehen yanka.
あんた運転でけへんやんか。
You can't drive, can you?

yanke やんけ (*janai ka* じゃないか)
Kantan yanke!
簡単やんけ！
It's easy, I'm telling you!

yarashii やらしい vulgar, disgusting (*iyarashii* 嫌らしい)

yaro やろ (*darō* だろう)
Ashita, yakyū suru yaro?
明日、野球するやろ？
We're playing baseball tomorrow, right?

yaru やる (See 54) give (*ageru* あげる)

yate やて (See 60) I heard that . . . (*datte* だって); I'm sure that . . .
(*da yo* だよ)

yatcha やっちゃ person, thing (*yatsu da* 奴だ)

yatta やった (*datta* だった)
Kinō no shiai, dō yatta?

昨日の試合、どうやった？

How was yesterday's game?

yattara やったら (*dattara* だったら)

Ame yattara, kyanpu chūshi yana.

雨やったら、キャンプ中止やな。

If it rains, camping is cancelled, right?

yossha よっしゃ (See 55) yes, okay, great

yō よう (See 24) very, much, often, well (*yoku* よく)

yōke ようけ (See 39) a lot, many (*takusan* 沢山)

yōsan ようさん (See 39) a lot, many (*takusan* 沢山)

yū 言う, ゆう (See 25) to speak (*iu* 言う)

yūta 言うた said (*itta* 言った)

Kakarichō ga sō yūtan?

係長がそう言うたん？

Did the manager say so?

yūte 言うて (See 25) to say; *-te* form (*itte* 言って)

zukkoi ずっこい (See 40) cunning, sneaky (*zurui* ずるい, *warugashikoi* 悪賢い)

▪ Index ▪

The first appearance of main word entries and their dictionary appearance are indicated in boldface type.